Earth Heroes

Champions of Wild Animals

By Carol L. and Bruce Malnor
Illustrations by Anisa Claire Hovemann

DAWN Publications

To our parents, Robert and Connie Malnor & Elmer and Illa Lattimer, with gratitude and love.—CLM and BRM

For all the animals. —ACH

Copyright © 2010 Carol and Bruce Malnor
Illustration copyright © 2010 Anisa Claire Hovemann
All rights reserved.

Library of Congress Cataloging-in-Publication Data

Malnor, Carol.
  Earth heroes : champions of wild animals / by Carol L. and Bruce Malnor ; illustrated by Anisa Claire Hovemann. -- 1st ed.
    p. cm.
  Summary: "The youth, career, and lasting contributions of some of the world's greatest naturalists and environmentalists are featured in this series of books on champions of the wilderness, ocean, and wild animals, with this volume focusing on those who saved wild animal species from extinction"--Provided by the publisher.
  Includes bibliographical references and index.
  ISBN 978-1-58469-123-5 (pbk.)
 1. Wildlife conservationists--Biography--Juvenile literature. 2. Naturalists--Biography--Juvenile literature. 3. Endangered species--Juvenile literature. I. Malnor, Bruce. II. Hovemann, Anisa Claire, ill. III. Title. IV. Title: Champions of wild animals.
  QL83.M315 2010
  333.95'4160922--dc22
  [B]
                              2010016030

Printed in U.S.A.
10 9 8 7 6 5 4 3 2 1
First Edition

Book design and computer production by Patty Arnold, *Menagerie Design and Publishing*.

Printed on recycled paper

Dawn Publications
12402 Bitney Springs Road
Nevada City, CA 95959
530-274-7775
nature@dawnpub.com

TABLE OF CONTENTS

Introduction: *Who's Wild About Animals?*   4

William Temple Hornaday: *Brought Wildlife to Millions*   6
1854–1937

Jay Norwood "Ding" Darling: *A Duck's Best Friend*   22
1876–1962

Rachel Carson: *The Scientist Who Wouldn't Be Silent*   38
1907–1964

Roger Tory Peterson: *The World's Foremost Birder*   54
1908–1996

Ronald "RD" Lawrence: *Friend of the Wolf*   70
1921–2003

Edward O. Wilson: *Lord of the Ants*   86
1929–present

Jane Goodall: *Ambassador for Wild Chimps*   102
1934–present

The Douglas-Hamilton Family: *A Family Saving Elephants*   120
1933, 1942, 1970—present

Conclusion: *Become a Hero!*   136

About the Authors and Illustrator   139

Sources and Credits   140

Index   142

Who's WILD About Animals?

What are your favorite wild animals? Lions and tigers and bears? With over one million species in the Animal Kingdom, there are lots to choose from. They include the tiniest ants, less than a sixteenth of an inch long, and the largest land animals in the world, African elephants twenty-five feet long. Wild animals are defined as animals that live in their natural settings. They are found all over the world, from cold polar regions to steamy tropical jungles.

This book introduces you to eight people—Earth Heroes who discovered their favorite wild animals and dedicated their lives to studying and protecting them. Bison and birds, chimps and seals, wolves and elephants all owe their survival to the people described in these pages. And the personal life of each hero is as unique as the animals they've protected.

William Hornaday hunted animals for many years, but was so saddened by the senseless destruction of the American bison that he stopped hunting and saved it from extinction.

Rachel Carson was severely criticized in newspapers and on television for her book warning about the dangers of DDT. But by daring to speak up, countless species of animals were saved.

Birds fascinated **Roger Tory Peterson** and **Ding Darling**. Both of these men used their creativity and artistic talents to spark others' interest in birds too.

Ron Lawrence loved sea creatures as a boy and discovered the love of wolves in Canada as an adult. His stories corrected myths about wolves.

A childhood accident forced **Ed Wilson** to focus on the little creatures of the world. This focus helped him make a major scientific discovery about ants when he was only thirteen.

Jane Goodall's first toy was a stuffed chimpanzee, and she grew up to discover the secrets of the chimp's world.

Virgo, a full-grown African elephant, greeted **Saba Douglas-Hamilton** when she was just three months old. Saba joined her family in their life's work of saving elephants.

Ron Lawrence reminds us, "To know animals, one must know the land." Wild animals depend on the land. The health of the habitat determines their health. The health of wildlife greatly influences the health of the habitat itself. Everything is interconnected. It's like two sides of the same coin. One side shows us how the dying habitat in Yellowstone National Park was revived once wolves were reintroduced. And the other side of the coin shows us how the creation of wildlife refuges allowed ducks to thrive.

John Muir, of *Champions of the Wilderness*, wrote, "When we try to pick out anything by itself, we find it hitched to everything else in the Universe." This is true for the multitude of interconnections between the wilderness and wildlife. And it's also true for the *Earth Heroes* series: *Champions of the Wilderness*, *Champions of the Ocean*, and *Champions of Wild Animals*. Each book relates to the other two. Here are a few of the connections among the champions:

- **Teddy Roosevelt** and **Margaret Murie** helped preserve American wilderness as national parks for both people and animals. **Eugenie Clark** helped preserve a coral reef in Egypt as a national park so it could remain a safe haven for a thousand species of fish.
- **Jane Goodall** became a crusader for wilderness preservation when she realized how much rain forest had been cut down in Tanzania. **Wangari Maathai** organized the Green Belt movement to plant trees in Kenya.
- **Aldo Leopold** taught ecology in the 1940s, and **Ed Wilson** teaches ecology today.

The interconnections of these people are like the web of life itself. **Sylvia Earle** sums it up: "We are all together in this single living ecosystem called planet earth." How fortunate we are to have so many heroes working to save the wilderness, oceans, and animals. **David Suzuki** states:

> We are the earth, through the plants and animals that nourish us.
>
> We are the rains and the oceans that flow through our veins.
>
> We are human animals, related to all life . . .

As you read the remarkable stories in *Earth Heroes* you become an important part of the connection too.

Earth Heroes: Champions of Wild Animals

William Temple Hornaday
1854—1937

The Man Who Brought Wildlife to Millions

"No civilized nation should allow its wild animals to be exterminated."

Twenty-year-old William peered out from his hiding place among the mangrove roots. He was anxiously waiting for "Ole Boss," an enormous crocodile he had discovered along a Florida creek. Ole Boss had eluded him for two days, but William was determined to add this unique specimen to his wildlife collection.

Suddenly, Ole Boss appeared in the middle of the creek. William took aim and fired his rifle, hitting the crocodile directly in the eye. Crazed with pain, the crocodile thrashed and rolled in the water. It dove to the bottom of the creek and then shot straight up out of the water, tail first.

Amidst the chaos, William yelled to his friend Chester Jackson who was waiting in a canoe upstream. With all his might, Chester plunged his fish spear into the crocodile's side. But Ole Boss easily snapped off the spear's handle and escaped downstream. Despite the danger, William jumped into the canoe and paddled in wild pursuit. After several more gun shots, Ole Boss was finally driven onto the shore. William had his prize specimen! The next day he killed a female crocodile, probably Ole Boss' mate.

William Hornaday is now celebrated as a wildlife conservation hero. How could he kill Ole Boss—and many other animals as well? The answer is found in history. In the past, scientists killed animals in order to study them. And wildlife collectors like William played an important role in scientific discovery. Some famous collectors of that era included Charles Darwin, John James Audubon, and Teddy Roosevelt.

When William discovered Ole Boss in 1875, he made a major contribution to science. At that time, scientists believed that *only* alligators, *not* crocodiles, existed in the U.S. But Ole Boss proved them wrong!

William had not only collected the first two crocodiles found in the United States, he had also discovered a brand new species of crocodile. In a scientific paper he wrote about the crocodiles, he named the species *Crocodilus floridanus*. The two crocodiles caused a public sensation when they were displayed at the 1876 World's Fair and later at the Smithsonian Institution's National Museum.

At the age of twenty, William had achieved his first career goal: to become a professional naturalist and writer. And throughout his long life, he made many contributions to science and nature.

William was born in Plainfield, Indiana, in 1854. When he was two years old, his family moved to Iowa. As a very young child he roamed the prairie, creeks, and forests that surrounded his family's farm. He became aware of the "wild beauty" of nature and delighted in the "persistent and tireless singing" of song sparrows, the great flocks of passenger pigeons that swept the sky, and the "graceful gyrations" of the fork-tailed kites.

He loved all animals! And when he was nine years old, he learned an important lesson about killing them. It was summertime, and he was visiting his aunt and uncle in Indiana. Several noisy blue jays had taken over the cherry trees in his uncle's backyard. They were squawking loudly, and his uncle said, "Billy, I wish you would take some stones and kill some of those confounded jaybirds."

Wishing to please his uncle, William went outside and started throwing stones. On his fourth try, he hit one of blue jays and killed it.

At first he was proud of his success. But when he picked up the dead bird, he noticed it was really beautiful, with "gorgeous blue, black, and white plumage and a saucy crest." His pride was replaced with sadness and regret as he realized that no one would ever enjoy its loveliness again. By killing the jay, he had wasted its beauty.

Another strong influence in William's young life was his family's enthusiasm for reading. Many evenings they all gathered around the lamp and took turns reading aloud to one another. William's favorite books were about travel and adventure, explorers and heroes. He imagined himself going to new lands, discovering exotic animals, and performing heroic deeds.

All of William's childhood dreams came true! As a young man he traveled to many far-away places in search of rare and unusual species. Through taxidermy he preserved their beauty. Later in his life he became a hero for wildlife, saving many animals from extinction.

The Civil War brought an end to his happy and carefree childhood. One brother was killed and two were crippled fighting in the war. His parents struggled to keep their farm going. They worked so hard they became ill and died. By the time William was fourteen he was an orphan.

For a while he lived with various relatives, working on their farms and caring for large herds of cattle and sheep. His half-brother

Killing a blue jay taught William an important lesson about the beauty of animals.

was especially kind to him, but when William turned sixteen he decided it was time to choose his own career.

He didn't like farming. He preferred reading and writing, so he decided to get a job as a newspaper editor. He confidently applied for positions at two local papers. To his surprise, he was turned down by both of them. But William wasn't easily discouraged. The rejections taught him a lesson. He realized he needed to get more education.

In 1871 he enrolled at Oskaloosa College. His plan was to improve his writing skills. But an unexpected event changed his life's direction—his first lesson in taxidermy. Taxidermy is the art of skinning a dead animal and stuffing it to make it look alive. He was hooked!

He had an opportunity to try taxidermy on one of his own specimens the following year when he attended Iowa Agricultural College (now called Iowa State University). With his usual confidence, William stuffed and mounted a squirrel. He proudly presented it to the president of the college, hoping to be rewarded for his work. Instead, the president took one look at it and called it a "monstrosity."

William didn't give up. He next tried taxidermy on a white pelican. The bird was huge—bigger than he was—with a wingspan of over nine feet! At first he was nervous. But his zoology professor, Dr. Charles Bessey, came to his aid by giving him *Birds of America* by John James Audubon. Using Audubon's painting as a guide, William successfully created a life-like stuffed pelican. The university displayed William's pelican for many years.

Dr. Bessey became a friend as well as a teacher, and he continued to support William's passion for taxidermy. He helped him get a job in New York at Ward's Natural Science Establishment, a company that supplied museums with specimens of birds, mammals, and reptiles. Some of the best taxidermists in the world worked there.

On November 18, 1873, at the age of nineteen, William left Iowa to begin a new life and career. It was while working for Ward's Establishment that William successfully collected Ole Boss, the crocodile specimen.

William quickly learned taxidermy as well as other skills needed by a collector-naturalist. He became a trusted employee, and in 1877 he was sent around the world on a collecting trip. He had one thrilling adventure after another as he traveled across Europe, Africa, and Southeast Asia. Today, many thousands of people have seen the museum specimens William collected on this trip.

One of the last stops of the trip was Borneo. He was the first American naturalist to visit this large island. Despite the challenge of slogging through mud and ooze a foot deep, William appreciated Borneo's spectacular scenery—tree trunks covered in beautiful orchids, fresh water dripping off green leaves, and brilliantly-colored butterflies.

While in Borneo, William had the rare opportunity to observe orangutans in their natural environment. He saw them gather sticks to build nests, hold their babies to nurse them, and fight other orangutans to defend their territory. He marveled at how human-like they sometimes seemed, especially when they used their hands to drink water or when they snored while sleeping.

Watching the orangutans go about their daily lives inspired William to create a new kind of museum display—a "habitat group display." The first display he created of this type was called "A Fight in the Treetops." It showed two males fighting over territory. The males bared their teeth as they fiercely glared at each other. Several females and babies watched the fight as they hung

William's creative orangutan display, "A Fight in the Treetops," revolutionized how museums exhibited wildlife.

from nearby branches. William's second display, "Orang at Home," depicted a peaceful family scene. The orangutans relaxed in the treetops just the way William had seen them in Borneo.

Today, all American museums use habitat group displays. But museums were very different in 1878. Animals were displayed alone in small glass cases. They were labeled with Latin names. Scientists visited museums, but most people found it extremely boring to look at row upon row of glass cases.

William thought museums should be interesting places where the general public could learn about natural history. His habitat group displays told stories about the lives of Borneo's orangutans. They showed what the animals looked like, where they lived, what they ate, and how they behaved. People had never seen anything like these displays before, and they loved them!

William also wanted his displays to show the orangutans' power and grace. But in order to do that, he needed to invent new taxidermy methods. He experimented with wooden manikins and clay to sculpt muscle and make lifelike facial expressions. Using both artistic skills and scientific knowledge, William worked hard to perfect his techniques. His results were so good that other taxidermists used them too. He completely changed how taxidermy was done in America.

By 1882 William had earned a reputation as one of the most skilled taxidermists in the United States. He was offered the prestigious job as Chief Taxidermist for the Smithsonian Institution's Natural History Museum. Although William was grateful for everything he had learned at Ward's Establishment, he was excited to start his new job in Washington, D.C. His first assignment was to restore two crocodile displays. They were the same two crocodiles he had captured in Florida seven years earlier!

In the midst of his busy life as a collector and taxidermist, William married Josephine Chamberlain. They had a long and happy marriage.

In 1880 William used his new realistic taxidermy techniques to show a tiger's power and grace.

He said that her independent spirit and accomplishments as a teacher inspired him to achieve many of his own successes.

One of his successes was writing a book about his worldwide collecting trip, *Two Years in the Jungle: The Experiences of a Hunter and Naturalist in India, Ceylon, the Malay Peninsula and Borneo*. People loved reading his adventurous tales of faraway places and exotic animals. This book, along with nature stories he wrote for newspapers and magazines, made him a popular author.

While working at the National Museum, William became aware that herds of American bison were rapidly disappearing. The bison, also called the American buffalo, was North America's largest land animal. William wanted to make sure that museums across the country had specimens of this magnificent creature before it became extinct.

In 1886, he led a bison collecting expedition to Montana. William brought back twenty-five bison skins—some of the last wild bison in

America. He used all of his skills to create two bison exhibits. Not only were they beautiful, they also taught people about why the bison was on the brink of extinction.

With the bison displays he created, William reached the highest point in his profession as a taxidermist. But he was haunted by the millions of bison skulls and skeletons he saw lying across the Montana plains. William knew he no longer wanted to preserve dead animals. He would devote his life to keeping them alive!

William published a book about the history of bison titled *The Extermination of the American Bison* in 1887. It marked the beginning of his crusade for wildlife conservation. He provided facts and figures that people didn't generally know. For example, the American bison was once the most numerous species of mammal in the world. In 1800, there were over 60 million bison roaming the prairies and plains of North America. But by 1889, there were only 1,095 bison left on the face of the Earth.

The Extermination of the American Bison also suggested some hope for the future. William thought that if people knew about the useless destruction of the bison, they might want to help save other threatened species.

William's book had a huge impact. Americans were beginning to take an interest in the environment. During the late 1800s and early 1900s, President Theodore "Teddy" Roosevelt established five new national parks, expanded national forests, and created the first bird sanctuary (see *Earth Heroes: Champions of the Wilderness*). Many different types of environmental organizations were also forming, including the Boone and Crockett Club for sportsmen and the Audubon Society for birdwatchers. William also started a conservation organization called the Campfire Club of America.

Just like John Muir, Teddy Roosevelt, and Aldo Leopold (see *Earth Heroes: Champions of the Wilderness*), William believed that natural resources, including wildlife, should be saved simply because nature was beautiful and interesting. For many years he worked passionately to save the bison, not because they could be used in any practical way, but because he loved and appreciated them.

William joined Teddy Roosevelt and other pioneering environmentalists to form the American Bison Society. They convinced the federal government to establish the National Bison Range in Montana. William raised $10,000 to buy a small herd of bison for the new range and helped establish other ranges as bison habitat. His efforts to save the bison were successful! By 1918, the American bison was no longer in danger of extinction.

While William was writing *The Extermination of the American Bison*, he was also working to establish a zoological park that would provide a safe refuge for bison. He had rescued a bison calf on his collecting expedition and had brought it back to raise in captivity. He reasoned that if bison were protected, a zoological park could breed them and eventually reintroduce bison back into the wild. He also wanted to save other vanishing species like antelope, mountain goat, and bighorn sheep.

The Smithsonian Institution was willing to put William's idea to the test. They established a Department of Living Animals and put William in charge. In 1887, William went on another collecting trip—this time for *live* animals. Traveling by train through Dakota, Montana, and Washington Territories, he collected a variety of wild animals including a cinnamon bear, a white-tailed deer, two spotted

William established a zoo to protect American bison and other species. Here he stands with a baby he named "Sandy."

lynx, and four prairie dogs. William took good care of the animals and even slept with them at night. The only animal that caused him any difficulties was a badger that he kept below his bed. It kept trying to dig through the wall of the train car at night.

When William arrived back in Washington, D.C., the newspapers delighted readers with stories of his animals. They reported on the bald eagle with a broken wing and an escaped fox that led several men, boys, and dogs on a wild chase through city streets before it was captured.

As the public became aware of the "little try-out zoo" next to the Smithsonian Institution, they began to make animal donations. One of the first came from President Cleveland and his wife. They donated a golden eagle they had received as a Christmas present. Mrs. Cleveland also donated a spotted fawn she received from the State of New York. She was keenly interested in the zoo and quite frequently "drove down to the Smithsonian grounds from the White House with her friends to look after her fawn and to see the other animals."

It took years, but finally in 1889 Congress officially established the Smithsonian Institution's National Zoological Park, to be located in Washington, D.C.'s beautiful Rock Creek Valley. William was relieved. His animals desperately needed more room. He had already drawn up detailed plans for the zoo and was anxious to start building better facilities for them.

William's vision for the zoo was ahead of its time. In his plan, animals would roam freely in wide-open spaces instead of being confined behind barred cages. He thought this kind of open design would be more educational for zoo visitors because they would get a sense of the animals' natural habitat and behavior. This type of zoo design is now called a *biopark*.

But just as William was ready to start building, a new director of the Smithsonian Institution informed him that he wasn't going to use William's zoo design. William was surprised. He was even more shocked when the director told him that he was limiting William's decision-making authority and was going to hire a new zoo superintendent.

Even though William was dedicated to the zoo, he wasn't willing to compromise his principles. He resigned. Many years later he wrote in his unpublished autobiography that leaving the National Zoo was the best thing that could have happened to him. It pushed him into a new direction and opened up new opportunities.

He worked as a businessman for six years, but he never lost his love for animals. Then in 1896 he got a second chance to build the zoo of his dreams. The New York Zoological Society (now called the Wildlife Conservation Society) hired him to become the director of the New York Zoological Park, commonly known as the Bronx Zoo.

William Hornaday at the biopark he created in 1920, now called the Bronx Zoo.

William had complete freedom to create "the first true zoological park in the world." Large, open areas allowed the animals to live "under conditions most closely approximating those with which nature usually surrounds them." And the zoo also served as a miniature wildlife refuge for animals threatened with extinction. William said, "No civilized nation should allow its wild animals to be exterminated" without trying to preserve them.

Under thirty years of William's supervision, the Bronx Zoo became one of the largest and finest zoos in the world. It was the first zoo to hire a full-time veterinarian and establish a modern animal hospital. For many years the directors of new zoos from all over the United States came to William for advice.

While directing the zoo, William continued his "war for wildlife." He hired a researcher to survey the condition of wildlife across the United States and in Alaska. The results showed that wild birds and mammals were being hunted at an alarming rate.

As he did with the American bison, William sounded the alarm! He used his writing skills to rally public interest in protecting birds and other animals. In 1913 he wrote *Our Vanishing Wildlife*, followed by twenty more books and hundreds of newspaper and magazine articles. He stated the problems in ways that people could understand, and then he explained practical solutions.

William worked tirelessly to influence politicians to pass wildlife conservation laws. From 1909 to 1912 he led a campaign to get the federal government to save the Alaskan fur seal. The seals spent their summers on the Pribilof Islands in the Bering Sea. Hunters from the United States, as well as from Canada, Russia, and Japan, were hunting the seals to extinction. Due to William's efforts, the Fur Seal Treaty was signed in 1911.

Birds were another casualty of over-hunting. Thousands of shorebirds, songbirds, and game birds were sold to restaurants for food. Even robins! "Plume hunters" killed birds for their long, lacey feathers, which were used to decorate ladies' hats. Ounce for ounce, white egret feathers were worth more than gold in the 1880s, and these beautiful birds were hunted almost to extinction. William helped pass the Migratory Bird Act, which saved 1,200 species and millions of birds from slaughter.

In 1913, he created the Permanent Wild Life Protection Fund. He raised $105,000 and used the interest on the money to support conservation efforts around the country. Through the Fund, William established the Wildlife Protection Medal. It was given to people who promoted the protection of wildlife and wildlife habitat. After William's death the medal was renamed the Hornaday Medal and is now awarded through the Boy Scouts of America. The Hornaday Medal is the oldest conservation award given in the United States.

William retired from the zoo in 1926 at the age of 76, but continued his fight for wildlife. One of his fiercest battles was to decrease the waterfowl *bag limit*, the number of birds that could be killed per day. Some hunters were killing over a hundred a day. But the conservationists and preservationists couldn't agree on a new limit. Finally, after a decade of arguing, the bag limit was lowered from twenty-five ducks and ten geese per day to fifteen ducks and four geese per day. (It has since been lowered to four ducks and two geese per day.)

William died on March 6, 1937, just a few months after writing a long letter to President Franklin D. Roosevelt urging him to do more to protect wildlife.

He is remembered as a man of vision and creativity who loved animals and did more than any person of his time to protect wildlife. He brought wildlife to millions through the museum displays and zoo exhibits he created.

He received many honors. The National Wildlife Federation inducted him into its Conservation Hall of Fame. Hornaday Peak in Yellowstone National Park was named after him. In remembering his many honors, biographer James Andrew Dolph said,

> The most fitting memorials are the living ones—the bison and antelope which still can be found in the West, the V-shaped formations of ducks and geese across the autumn sky, and the fur seals on the far-off islands of Alaska.

FAST FACTS

Born: December 1, 1854, Plainfield, Indiana
Died: March 6, 1937, Stamford, Connecticut
Wife: Josephine Chamberlain

ACCOMPLISHMENTS:
- Saved the American buffalo (bison) from extinction
- Saved the Alaska fur seal from extinction
- Influenced the passage of laws and treaties that saved egrets, ducks, and other migratory birds from extinction
- Revolutionized how museums displayed wildlife exhibits
- Created the National Zoological Park
- Created New York Zoological Park, the first true biological park (now called the Bronx Zoo)
- Wrote numerous books including *The Extermination of the American Buffalo* and *Our Vanishing Wildlife*
- Established the Wildlife Protection Medal
- Inducted into National Wildlife Federation's Conservation Hall of Fame

RIPPLES OF INFLUENCE:

Famous People Who Influenced William Hornaday
John James Audubon, John Muir, President Theodore Roosevelt, Dr. Charles Bessey, Henry Augustus Ward

Famous People Influenced by William Hornaday
President Theodore Roosevelt, President and Mrs. Grover Cleveland, Aldo Leopold, and members of national organizations such as the Smithsonian Institution, United States Congress, and the Boy Scouts of America.

TIMELINE

William Hornaday's Life		Historical Context
Born December 1	1854	
	1860	U.S. Civil War begins
	1862	Ward's Estab. opens; Thoreau dies
	1865	Lincoln assassinated
First taxidermy lesson at college	1872	Yellowstone becomes 1st national park
Begins working for Ward's	1873	
Kills Ole Boss in Florida	1875	
	1876	Telephone invented; Ding Darling born
Travels on worldwide collecting trip	1877-1878	Phonograph patented; Wm. Beebe born
Marries Josephine	1879	Incandescent electric light invented
Chief Taxidermist of US Nat'l Museum	1882-1890	
	1887	Aldo Leopold born
Publishes *Extermination of Buffalo*	1889	
Creates NY Zoological Park	1896	
	1903	Wright Brothers fly plane
Co-founds American Bison Society	1905	Audubon Society formed
	1907	Rachel Carson born
	1908	Roger Peterson born; first Model T car
	1910	Boy Scouts of America established
Helps pass Fur Seal Treaty	1911	
Creates Wild Life Protection Fund	1913	John Muir loses battle for Hetch Hetchy
	1914	Passenger pigeon becomes extinct
	1917	U. S. enters WWI
Helps pass Migratory Bird Act	1918	
	1919	Theodore Roosevelt dies
	1921	R.D. Lawrence born
Retires from NY Zoological Park	1926	
Creates Bird Study merit badge (scouts)	1929	Stock market crash; E.O. Wilson born
Helps lower the bag limit for ducks	1930	Worldwide depression begins
	1933	Oria Douglas-Hamilton born
	1934	Jane Goodall born; "Dust Bowl" storms
Dies March 6	1937	
Peak named for him in Yellowstone NP	1938	

Jay Norwood "Ding" Darling
1876–1962

A Duck's Best Friend

"So go the ducks; so goes man."

Jay and his brother Frank rode their high-spirited Indian ponies through the tall prairie grass. Jay was as wild and free as the wilderness. His "backyard" was the South Dakota prairie, just across the Missouri River from his boyhood home in Sioux City, Iowa.

In the 1880s, the prairie was lush and unspoiled. Jay immersed himself in its beauty. He wandered through marshes filled with ducks and hillsides covered in wildflowers. He searched for coyotes, fox, and badgers that hid in the never-ending waves of grass. And on warm summer nights he camped by the river and listened to the growling "voice of the puma" as it crept along the riverbank.

When he became a teenager his summers of freedom ended. He had to work. Some summers he worked on his Uncle John's farm in Albion, Michigan. He got up early every morning to milk the cows; then he spent the day in the fields. Swinging a sharp scythe back and forth, he mowed marsh hay for hours. Other days he cut and gathered wheat by hand, going into corners of the field that the McCormick reaping machine couldn't reach.

Although the work was hard, Jay thought the farm was "paradise." He loved fishing in the creek. He delighted in the chorus of songbirds that greeted him as he walked through the fields.

Lots of ducks landed on the millpond, and sometimes Uncle John took over Jay's chores and sent him off hunting "to get a mess of ducks for dinner." But when Jay killed a duck during nesting time, his uncle "blistered his rear." Jay always remembered this first lesson in conservation: only hunt during the appropriate season. His uncle could never have guessed that Jay would grow up to teach the whole country about conservation and become known as "a duck's best friend."

The summers that Jay didn't go to his uncle's farm, he herded cattle on the prairie for anyone who would hire him. His love of nature deepened as he watched huge flocks of golden plover fill the sky and searched for prairie chickens hiding in thickets along the creeks. As an adult he wrote about the natural beauty he had observed: "My mind was filled with pictures which have never been erased."

Jay left home for college in Yankton, South Dakota. His goal was to prepare himself for medical school and to become a doctor. At age seventeen, he was full of energy and mischief! After taking the college president's horse and carriage on a late-night "joy ride," Jay was expelled. But he didn't give up his plans to become a doctor.

The following year, 1895, Jay enrolled at Beloit College in Wisconsin. With an outgoing personality and lots of personal charm, Jay was a natural leader. He liked to take charge. He became the manager of the track team, editor of the college newspaper, leader of the glee club, and art director for the college yearbook.

Working on the yearbook gave Jay an opportunity to show off his talent for drawing. From the time he saw his first illustrated card as a little boy, Jay was fascinated with drawing. His family thought drawing was "wicked" and called it "a waste of time." But young Jay kept drawing anyway. Keeping a pad of paper and a pencil in his pocket, he made quick sketches whenever he had an opportunity.

The college yearbook offered a particularly good opportunity for Jay to combine his artistic flair with his wry sense of humor. He drew exaggerated caricatures of the college faculty in ridiculous situations. One professor was drawn to look like the devil shoveling students into a furnace. Another was sketched as a male ballet dancer wearing a tutu. Jay even drew likenesses of the entire faculty pictured as a line of chorus girls.

He signed his yearbook drawings "D'ing," which was a contraction of his last name. The apostrophe stood for the letters "a," "r," and "l," which he left out in order to make his signature look funnier. Within a few years, this signature became famous and hundreds of thousands of people around the country knew him affectionately as "Ding."

Like the mustang he rode as a boy, Ding was high-spirited. Personal freedom and exciting experiences were important—more important to him than his studies. During his junior year Ding failed every class except biology. He was suspended for a year.

Although Ding described himself as "a no-good student," he had a sharp intellect and could easily learn anything that interested him. With his goal to become a doctor, it's not surprising that the classes he was most interested in were the life sciences. His biology teacher opened his eyes to see human life as part of a bigger reality. Although the word "ecology" didn't exist at the time, Ding grew to understand that all life was connected. He realized that human life was interwoven with the "plants and animals with which it shares Earth's soil, water, and air."

Although Ding never became a doctor, he remained devoted to preserving all life.

Ding eventually graduated in 1900 and took a job as a reporter for the *Journal*, a Sioux City newspaper. While there, he wrote an interesting and amusing article about a courtroom trial. One of the lawyers caused a lot of excitement in the courtroom with his wild gestures and animated behavior. Ding's editor wanted a photograph of the lawyer to go along with the article. Knowing that the lawyer always refused to have his photo taken, Ding secretly snuck up on him. But when the lawyer spotted Ding with his camera, he let out a whoop, jumped over a chair, and took off after Jay swinging his cane. Ding narrowly escaped a strike to his head and skedaddled down the street.

Since he didn't get the photo, Ding instead gave his editor a sketch of the agitated lawyer he had doodled while watching the trial. It was published, and Ding's career as a cartoonist was born.

His first regular series of cartoons, called "Local Snapshots," featured caricatures of well-known Sioux City citizens. People loved seeing their friends and neighbors drawn in Ding's humorous style! His next assignment was illustrating a column called "Interviews That Never Happened." Ding's sketches gently poked fun at many community leaders—something he continued to do for fifty years.

Ding's busy job at the newspaper didn't stop him from enjoying his favorite outdoor pastimes. After putting in a full day's work at the *Journal*, he would head out of town with a horse and wagon to hunt and fish along the Missouri River. Then he'd race back just in time to cover the latest news stories and draw a cartoon.

In 1900, Ding drew his first *political* cartoon. It was about the upcoming presidential election in which he pictured Theodore "Teddy" Roosevelt and William McKinley riding atop an elephant (the symbol of the Republican Party). They won the election, and Roosevelt became one of Ding's favorite subjects as well as a good friend. Ding's most famous cartoon commemorated Roosevelt's death in 1919. It showed the "Rough Rider" astride his horse, waving goodbye with his cowboy hat in his hand.

Ding enthusiastically agreed with Roosevelt's conservation views (see *Earth Heroes: Champions of the Wilderness*) and drew his first *conservation* cartoon in 1901 to support Roosevelt's campaign to establish a forestry service. Roosevelt was committed to saving the environment because he had witnessed the destruction of wild land he loved.

Ding, too, witnessed the destruction of a place he loved—his Uncle John's farm. Returning to the farm to attend his uncle's funeral, Ding was shocked by the sight that greeted him. It looked like the farm had died along with his uncle. A solitary crow flew up from a desolate barnyard. It was the only wildlife Ding saw—no songbirds, ducks, or fish. The river was a muddy trickle and the pond had dried up. The field where Ding had once plowed into eight inches of rich topsoil soil was stripped bare. The well was dry. The trees were cut down. Ding wrote about this shattering experience:

> This was my first conscious realization of what could happen to land, what could happen to clear running streams, what could happen to bird life and human life when the common laws of Mother Nature were disregarded . . . It was the disappearance of all that wonderful endowment of wild life [that] stirred my first instincts of conservation.

Ding worried that what had happened to his Uncle John's farm was happening all across the country. In the 1800s, when the rivers were deep and wildlife was abundant, settlers helped themselves to the riches of the land. They moved across the land cutting down all the trees, overgrazing the prairies, and killing many birds and animals. When they wore out one area, they moved on to another.

But the county's natural resources were limited. By the turn of the century, Roosevelt, Ding, and others were sounding the alarm. Americans needed to protect their environment! Roosevelt worked in government, establishing national parks, game preserves, and national forests. Ding

Ding used humorous images to convey environmental concerns.

worked in the newspaper business, drawing cartoons that increased people's awareness about conservation issues.

Over the years, his cartoons alerted people to environmental dangers such as clear-cutting forests, dumping waste into rivers, and hunting migrating birds. He was able to combine a serious message with a humorous or unusual image.

In a 1921 cartoon, Ding pictured the Earth as a little boy in a barber's chair. The little boy looks worried as the barber shaves all of the trees off of his head, leaving it bare. The title of the cartoon was "Wonder What Mother Will Say When She Finds He's Had It Clipped?"

Ding's cartoons appeared in nearly 150 newspapers across the country, and they had real impact. "What did Ding say today?" was a question heard on the bustling city street as well as at the farmer's kitchen table.

Newspapers played a key role in people's lives during the early 1900s. Papers not only were the primary source of news, they also included commentary *about* the news—editorials. A paper's editorials affected how its readers thought about issues and current events. Ding's editorial cartoons were especially powerful. They summarized complex issues and conveyed them with Ding's own humorous twist.

The boys who delivered the papers were some of Ding's biggest fans. "Even before unbundling the stacks of papers they were to deliver, carriers would crouch shivering in the dark, flashlight in hand, peering beneath the paper wrapping for a sneak preview of Ding's daily message."

In 1924 Ding received the highest award in journalism—the Pulitzer Prize. His prize-winning cartoon was titled "In the Good Old U.S.A."

It was a tribute to three Americans who had started out poor and become successful by their own efforts. The cartoon also warned young people not to "hang around street corners," clearly expressing Ding's values of self-reliance and hard work.

Ding often joked that no one believed drawing a cartoon was hard work. But it was! He began every day by reading at least six newspapers. Then he carefully chose an issue he thought was important. Ding's unique talent was making the issue easy to understand through a simple drawing. In describing his work he wrote, "Those few lines that appear in my pictures I only arrive at after hours and hours of work to simplify."

Ding had high standards for himself and others. When he heard about a young man who wanted to become a cartoonist, he cautioned, "If he is not willing to sacrifice . . . everything in order to devote himself to the development of his drawing ability, then he had better not try."

Although Ding spent a few years in New York City, he lived and worked most of his life in Iowa. He loved the people and the land. In 1932 he joined the Iowa State Fish and Game Commission to help make decisions about wildlife. He believed that wildlife management required trained professionals who could conduct research and make decisions based on scientific facts. But there just weren't enough people with that kind of training.

Ding came up with a creative solution to the problem—the establishment

Ding won two Pulitzer prizes and influenced many Americans with his editorial cartoons.

of the Cooperative Wildlife Research Unit to train wildlife scientists. In order to fund the research unit, he made a deal with the Iowa Fish and Game Commission and Iowa State College (now Iowa State University). These two institutions agreed to pay two-thirds of the program's costs for three years, and Ding used his own money to pay the final third, $9,000, which was a huge sum during the Great Depression. The research unit became a big success! Ding soon expanded it to nine more states, and today thirty-eight states have research units.

While Ding was focusing on wildlife in Iowa, the United States was in the grip of an ecological disaster. Enormous dust storms whipped across the plains. The sky turned black with dust. This environmental crisis was called the "Dust Bowl of the Thirties." It was a result of both natural and man-made events. For decades, farmers had plowed the prairie soil but failed to replenish it by rotating crops, leaving fields fallow, or planting cover crops. When a severe drought hit, it left the prairie dry. Without natural grasses to hold it in place, almost five billion tons of soil blew away. Bankrupt families had to pack up and leave their farms.

The Dust Bowl also devastated wildlife. Migrating birds, especially waterfowl such as ducks and geese, depended on the wetlands for food and nesting sites. But the wetlands were dry and the birds were dying out. To make matters worse, hunters shot birds in large numbers whenever they found them.

President Franklin D. Roosevelt (FDR) was keenly aware of the waterfowl problem and established a special "blue ribbon" conservation committee to study the issue and recommend solutions. The distinguished members of the committee were Aldo Leopold (see *Earth Heroes: Champions of the Wilderness*) Thomas Beck, and Ding. Leopold and Ding strongly believed that if wetland habitat were restored, the birds could make a comeback. Ding took charge, wrote the final report, and submitted it to FDR on February 8, 1934. One of the key recommendations was for the government to buy millions of acres of land to be restored as wildlife refuges.

Ding worked tirelessly to protect ducks and other waterfowl.

Jay Norwood "Ding" Darling

Just one month later the president asked Ding to become Chief of the Bureau of Biological Survey (now called the Fish and Wildlife Service), the government agency responsible for wildlife conservation.

Many people were shocked when Ding accepted the position. They couldn't understand why he would give up the freedom of his well-paid job as a cartoonist to work in the government at a drastically reduced salary. It was even more surprising that Ding, an outspoken Republican, would work for FDR, a Democrat. In addition, Ding had drawn many cartoons that were critical of FDR and his policies.

But Ding saw the job as a once-in-a-lifetime opportunity to make a difference in conservation. The Bureau of Biological Survey had excellent scientists working in the field, including dedicated people like Olaus Murie (see *Earth Heroes: Champions of the Wilderness*). However, the Survey had been poorly managed. It was bogged down and nothing was getting done. Ding took the job "temporarily" so that he could "shake things up" and get the Survey "back on the tracks."

And shake things up he did! Before his train arrived in Washington, D.C., he had already drawn up a plan to completely reorganize the entire Survey. But the changes didn't come easily. Not everyone liked his blunt way of speaking and acting, and he made some enemies who stood in his way. Moreover, the country was in the midst of the Great Depression. People were worried about finding jobs and feeding their families. They didn't care about ducks.

But Ding believed that the disappearance of any species warned about dangers ahead for mankind. He said, "So go the ducks; so goes man." And despite the difficulties, Ding was committed to helping wildlife. A whirlwind of energy, he pushed his ideas forward. In less than two years, Ding "broke the logjam" and got the Bureau of Biological Survey moving. People today continue to benefit from his many successes.

One of Ding's proudest accomplishments as Survey Chief was saving a wildlife refuge in Wyoming, the Shelton Antelope Refuge. At first sight he described it as "the most desolate piece of the American continent I ever visited." Local ranchers and herders were illegally grazing their cattle and sheep on the refuge land. It was bare and dry; all the grass was eaten down to the roots.

Ding immediately ordered a fence built around the entire refuge property. Once the land was protected, it quickly healed. By fall of the first year, the grass inside the fence had grown back enough to hold the winter snows. As the snow slowly melted in the spring, water soaked into the ground instead of running off. More grass grew the second year. Water stayed in the waterholes all summer, and the dry wells filled with water. The refuge thrived.

In addition to improving the existing 1.5 million acres of wildlife refuge land, Ding increased the system to 4.5 million acres. The expansion he began continued, and today the system includes more than 150 million acres and protects over 1,200 species of wildlife. Ding's original design of a flying blue goose remains the logo for the refuge system.

Another continuing success was Ding's creation of the Duck Stamp Program. It's often called one of the most effective conservation programs in history. All migratory waterfowl hunters are required to buy a Federal Duck Stamp and attach it to their hunting license. The money raised from the stamps goes toward protecting the ducks' natural habitat. Since Ding first began the Duck Stamp Program in 1934, $700 million has been raised to preserve over five million acres of wetlands. Ding used his artistic talents to design the first stamp for the program—two mallard ducks about to land on the water.

Not only did Ding save duck habitat, he enforced the tightest duck hunting restrictions in history. Historians have said that his actions prevented the "complete demise of continental waterfowl populations . . . He saved the day for ducks."

Ding had a special way of explaining complicated concepts by comparing them to something that was familiar. When he wanted to get all of the wildlife organizations to join together to increase their power, he said: "Eleven million horses running wild couldn't pull a rubber-tired baby buggy to town unless there was a harness to hook them to the load." Likewise, he insisted, eleven million sportsmen and 36,000 scattered sports groups "should have some kind of harness to band them together to exert a united influence for the good of wild life."

Ding gained support for his vision and was instrumental in forming the General Wildlife Federation, now called the National Wildlife Federation (NWF). He became its first president in 1936, and the federation remains an active force for conservation today. Two of NWF's magazines, *Ranger Rick* and *Your Big Backyard*, introduce wildlife to children at an early age. By the end of 1935 Ding felt that he had the Bureau of Biological Survey moving in the right direction. He resigned as chief and returned to Iowa to draw cartoons. He was awarded his second Pulitzer Prize in 1942 and retired from cartooning in 1949.

Ding firmly believed in education, especially conservation education. He worried that children were ignorant of the most important laws—the laws of nature. He gave speeches and wrote many magazine articles, like the excerpt from one below, explaining the importance of the environment:

> Ask anyone to name the three things he would rather have than anything else in the world, the first would probably be riches and the other two, more riches, which shows how little man knows what's good for him. If he had no air he would die in a few seconds, if he had no water he would die of thirst in a few days, and if there were no land he could have no food and would slowly die of starvation. But all three of these working together in the sunshine produce everything the richest man in the world can possess: food, clothing, forests, and all

the living creatures on earth. Leave out any one of the three and the other two are powerless to keep us alive.

Throughout Ding's life he suffered many serious illnesses and experienced several family tragedies. But with strong determination, Ding kept working for the cause of conservation. He died in 1962 at the age of 86. Ding's final cartoon, which he had drawn years earlier, appeared in newspapers the day after he died. Titled "Bye Now—It's Been Wonderful Knowing You," it depicted Ding rushing out of his office leaving a swirl of papers in his wake. His ever-present gun and fishing pole were stashed behind his couch.

Soon after his death, sixty friends, fans, and colleagues formed a foundation and helped establish the J.N. "Ding" Darling National Wildlife Refuge on Sanibel Island, Florida. It was the perfect tribute to Ding, who spent many happy days on the beaches of nearby Captiva Island with his family. Today over 800,000 visitors come to the refuge every year to canoe, kayak, fish, bird watch, and explore the trails. The plaque at the entrance to the refuge reads:

Ding and his son John enjoy a Florida beach.

> J. N. "Ding" Darling was a renowned cartoonist and ecologist whose perceptive mind, eloquent pen, and skilled brush endeared him to newspaper readers and conservationists during a long career, and a lifetime of ecological concern ... It was Darling's hope that future generations could share the beauty, serenity, and the bounty of nature he had known.

FAST FACTS

Born: October 21, 1876, Norwood, Michigan
Died: February 12, 1962, Des Moines, Iowa
Wife: Genevieve Pendleton
Children: John and Mary

ACCOMPLISHMENTS:
- Saved North American duck and waterfowl populations by creating refuges and drastically cutting waterfowl bag limits and seasons
- Revitalized and expanded the National Wildlife Refuge System and designed the system's "flying goose" symbol
- Created the Duck Stamp Program and designed the first stamp
- Helped create the National Wildlife Federation and served as its first president
- Devised successful ways to fund conservation programs at the local, state, and federal levels
- Established the Cooperative Wildlife Research Unit to train wildlife scientists
- Won two Pulitzer Prizes for his political cartoons in 1924 and 1942

RIPPLES OF INFLUENCE:

Famous People Who Influenced Ding Darling
Benjamin Franklin, Thomas Jefferson, J. J. Audubon, Samuel Adams, Theodore Roosevelt, and Gifford Pinchot

Famous People Influenced by Ding Darling
President Theodore Roosevelt, Aldo Leopold, President Franklin Roosevelt, and President Herbert Hoover

TIMELINE

Jay "Ding" Darling's Life		Historical Context
Born October 21 in Norwood, Michigan	1876	Telephone invented
	1879	Incandescent electric light invented
Moved to Sioux City, Iowa	1886	
	1887	Aldo Leopold born
Signs "DING" to yearbook drawing	1898	
Draws first political cartoon	1900	
Draws fist conservation cartoon	1901	Teddy Roosevelt becomes President
	1905	Audubon Society formed
Marries Genevieve Pendleton (Penny)	1906	
	1907	Rachel Carson born
	1908	Roger Peterson born: first Model T car
	1914	WW I begins
Syndicates cartoons via *Herald Tribune*	1917-1945	
	1919	Teddy Roosevelt dies
	1921	R. D. Lawrence born
Wins Pulitzer Prize for a cartoon	1924	
	1929	Stock market crash; E.O. Wilson born
	1930	Worldwide depression begins
Becomes Iowa Game Commissioner	1932	
	1933	Oria Douglas-Hamilton born
Becomes Chief of Bureau of Biological Survey; expands wildlife refuges; creates Duck Stamp Program	1934	"Dust Bowl" storms rage; William Beebe descends half a mile in bathysphere; Jane Goodall born
Founds Nat'l Wildlife Federation	1936	
	1937	William Hornaday dies
Wins Pulitzer Prize for a cartoon	1942	Iain Douglas-Hamilton born
	1945	WW II ends
Suffers from many health issues	1950s	
Dies February 12 in Iowa	1962	*Silent Spring* published
J. N. "Ding" Darling NWR established	1965	

Earth Heroes: Champions of Wild Animals

Rachel Carson
1907–1964

A Scientist Who Wouldn't Be Silent

"Those who dwell . . . among the beauties of the earth are never alone or weary in life."

Rachel knew she would be severely criticized and publicly ridiculed. Her hard-won scientific reputation would be smeared. Many people would call her a "crazy fanatic." Others would accuse her of being a Communist, lesbian, and traitor. She would stand alone to confront one of the most powerful industries in the country. But she did it anyway because she knew it was the *right* thing to do. What was her courageous action? Rachel dared to write a book called *Silent Spring*. In it, she told the truth about the devastation caused by DDT and other chemical pesticides.

The first chapter, "A Fable for Tomorrow," begins: "There once was town in the heart of America where all life lived in harmony with its surroundings." The fable describes beautiful scenes of crops growing in the fields, birds singing from the trees, and wildflowers splashing color along roadsides.

Then something dreadful happens! Birds disappear from the trees and fish float dead in the streams. Chickens lay eggs that don't hatch. Flowers appear on apple trees, but no fruit forms because there are no bees to pollinate the flowers. Wildflowers disappear, replaced by brown, lifeless stems. People get sick from unknown diseases. A strange silence falls over the land.

Rachel wrote, "No witchcraft, no enemy action had silenced the rebirth of new life in this stricken world. The people had done it to themselves." They had poisoned themselves and the land with chemicals, especially pesticides like DDT.

Although the town in the fable was fictitious, in 1962 similar disastrous events were actually happening in towns all across America. *Silent Spring* sounded the alarm and energized the modern environmental movement.

It was as if all of Rachel's life had set the stage for her to write this powerful and controversial book. Born in 1907, she was raised on a small farm in Springdale, Pennsylvania. Always curious about the world around her, Rachel delighted in exploring nature. When she wasn't doing her chores of gathering eggs, pumping water, or tending the garden, she "spent long days outdoors in fields and woods, happiest with the wild birds and creatures as companions." Her dog, Candy, eagerly tagged along on Rachel's outdoor adventures.

Rachel later wrote, "If a child is to keep alive his inborn sense of wonder, he needs the companionship of at least one adult who can share it, rediscovering with him the joy, excitement and mystery of the world we live in." For Rachel, that adult was her mother, Maria.

Maria loved and respected nature. She taught Rachel the names of the birds, insects, and wildflowers that lived around the farm. Rachel and her mother discovered a family of baby robins whose nest had been blown down by the wind. They brought the little birds home and raised them on their screened porch. Maria's reverence for animal life even included insects. Rachel often watched her mother carry a spider or bug outside and release it rather than kill it.

Maria also taught Rachel to love literature. Maria had been a teacher, and she created a home library in their farmhouse parlor. In the evening, the whole family would gather around the stove to listen as Maria read aloud. Rachel and her older sister and brother would be transported to far-off places and long-ago times.

Rachel loved to read, especially to her dog, Candy.

"I must go down to the sea again, to the lonely sea and the sky" is the opening line for one of Rachel's favorite poems, "Sea Fever," by John Masefield. The poem described exactly how Rachel felt. She yearned for the sea. Sometimes she would put a conch shell up to her ear and imagine she was standing on a beach listening to the sound of the ocean waves. Remembering her childhood desire for the ocean, Rachel recalled, "I dreamed of it and I longed to see it, and I read all the sea literature I could find."

Rachel began reading when she was just a toddler. The Beatrix Potter stories about Peter Rabbit, Squirrel Nutkin, Jemima Puddle-duck, and Benjamin Bunny captured her imagination. It's no wonder she started writing about bunnies, kittens, and birds. She illustrated her stories and made some of them into books, complete with book jackets. She even created miniature books that would fit into the palm of her hand.

In elementary school, Rachel was an "A" student and had good relationships with all of her teachers. But the other students considered her an outsider. It wasn't easy for Rachel to make friends, and she spent a lot of time alone or with her mother.

Rachel's quiet world of books and nature changed dramatically in 1917 when the United States entered World War I. Her older brother, Robert, became an Army pilot and went to fight in Europe against the Germans. Rachel worried about him and anxiously waited for his letters. One of Robert's letters inspired her to write a story she called "A Battle in the Clouds." It was about a brave, young Canadian pilot who earned the respect of the enemy with his expert flying skills.

Rachel submitted her story to *St. Nicholas*, a children's literary magazine. She waited and waited. Finally, after five months, her story appeared in the September 1918 issue. She was overjoyed. A published author at eleven years old! And to her great delight, her story earned her a *St. Nicholas* Silver Badge. Rachel later recalled, "I doubt that any royalty check of recent years has given me as great joy as the notice of that award."

Rachel kept writing stories and two more were published in *St. Nicholas*. One of them earned a Gold Badge and prize money of ten dollars—a big sum in those days. "Perhaps that early experience of seeing my work in print played its part in fostering my childhood dream of becoming a writer."

She was in good company. Several other famous authors had their writing published in *St. Nicholas* as children, including E. B. White, author of *Charlotte's Web* and *Stuart Little*. Rachel felt very satisfied with herself and was more certain than ever that she would spend her life as a writer.

She graduated in 1925 at the top of her class of twenty-eight girls and sixteen boys. Next to her yearbook photo a poem written by her classmates described her perfectly:

Rachel's like the mid-day sun,
Always very bright.
Never stops her studying
'Til she gets it right.

Maria did everything she could to scrape together enough money to send Rachel to college. She even sold the beautiful china and silver she had inherited from her mother. Her father promised to give the college part of their farmland. But even with Rachel's partial scholarship, they were still short. Fortunately, the college president recognized Rachel as an extremely gifted student. He stepped in and arranged for private donors to fund the remaining portion of her tuition.

Pennsylvania Women's College (now Chatham College) was only sixteen miles away in Pittsburgh, but it was a totally different world to Rachel. There were three hundred students and she was surrounded by constant activity. Living in a large dorm and sleeping and eating with so many other girls were brand new experiences for someone who was used to being all alone.

She spent most of her time going to classes and studying, and she also continued to write. Her articles and stories were published in the student newspaper and literary magazine. In one of her stories, Rachel wrote vividly about the sea's towering waves and the sound of the crashing breakers—sights and sounds she wouldn't experience for four more years.

Even though Rachel was in college, Maria was never far away. If Rachel didn't come home for the weekend, Maria traveled to the school, staying with Rachel in the dorm. Most of Rachel's classmates thought this quite strange. But Rachel didn't seem to object to her mother's involvement in her life. Their close relationship continued until Maria died in 1958 at the age of 90.

The school required that every student take a science class. When Rachel chose a biology class taught by Miss Mary Skinker, she had no idea it would be a major turning point in her life.

Rachel and Miss Skinker hit it off immediately. Rachel appreciated the high expectations that Miss Skinker held for her students. Miss Skinker appreciated Rachel's sharp intellect. Their relationship grew into a deep mutual friendship.

They spent many hours together outside of class discussing not only science, but also literature and art. They tromped through the woods and along streams. The love of nature that Rachel had known as

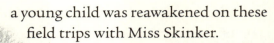

a young child was reawakened on these field trips with Miss Skinker.

Back at the lab, Rachel examined under a microscope the specimens they collected. She was fascinated by what she saw. As Rachel gained scientific knowledge of individual plants and animals, she developed an even deeper appreciation of nature as an indivisible whole.

Rachel had always thought of herself as a writer. But after discovering the world of biology, she started to think of herself as a scientist. A huge inner conflict developed. She felt she had to make a choice between her two passions: science and writing. Her decision was especially difficult because in 1927 science was closed to women. Women could be wives, mothers, and—if they were unmarried—they could be teachers. But like many other occupations, science was strictly for men.

Nevertheless, Rachel took the bold step of changing her major from English to biology. The college was abuzz with the shocking news. Students exclaimed: "How could she!" "Is she nuts?" "What does she think she's doing?" Even the college president, who saw great promise in Rachel's career as a writer or teacher, was upset and tried to persuade Rachel to change her mind. But Rachel was firm. She loved biology and was determined to become a scientist.

The change in majors meant Rachel had a lot of catching up to do. She dropped the English classes she loved in order to take several challenging science courses. Although she went to the junior prom, her demanding schedule left her little time for fun. She poured herself into her studies with her usual commitment to excellence.

As graduation approached, Rachel kept asking herself, "What should I do?" One night, as the wind and rain beat against her dorm window, she suddenly remembered a line from "Locksley Hall," by the famed poet Alfred Tennyson: "The mighty wind arises, roaring seaward, and I go." Suddenly it was clear. She would go to the sea. Recalling that night years later, Rachel said she felt the poem spoke directly to her, saying that "my own destiny was somehow linked to the sea."

Rachel graduated from college with high honors in 1929. Thanks to the recommendations of Miss Skinker and other college faculty, she was given two wonderful opportunities: a summer internship at Woods Hole Marine Biological Laboratory in Massachusetts and a full scholarship for graduate studies at the prestigious Johns Hopkins University.

On her way to Woods Hole, Rachel took a brief vacation with Miss Skinker in Maryland. The time sped by as they rode horses, hiked, and talked about life. Miss Skinker was Rachel's role model. The challenges Miss Skinker faced as a woman scientist, Rachel knew she would face too. Miss Skinker told Rachel she had broken off an earlier engagement because she didn't believe she could have both a marriage and a career. She felt she needed to be single-minded in the pursuit of her professional goals. Rachel felt the same way, and as it turned out, she also never married. When asked why not, she simply said, "No time."

Rachel's heart's desire was finally fulfilled when she arrived at Woods Hole. The glorious sea was all around her! In a letter to a friend, she wrote, "One can't walk very far in any direction without running into the ocean."

She had landed in a "biologist's paradise." She splashed in the waves and explored the tide pools. She held sea creatures and breathed in the fresh salty air as seagulls flew overhead.

Everything about Woods Hole suited her. The scientists were intellectuals as she was, and for the first time in her life she fit in! Biographer Marty Jezer states,

At Woods Hole she discovered a community of people who shared a passion for science and the sea. After work, they often gathered—at a picnic on the beach or over coffee in the dining hall—to share their theories, aspirations, and delight in working and living in so interesting an environment. Rachel Cason had found her niche.

Exhilarated, it became clear to her that she should become a marine biologist. Rachel learned that Elmer Higgins at the U.S. Bureau of Fisheries (now called the U.S. Fish and Wildlife Service) was a good person to consult about careers in marine biology. Always eager to talk to an expert, she asked him about job possibilities. He was brutally honest. There were jobs for men, but *not* for women. That's just the way it was. He suggested she go into teaching.

Rachel was just as honest with Mr. Higgins. She did *not* want to be a teacher. She wanted be a *scientist*. Her firm manner and quiet determination impressed Higgins, and he told her to see him again when she completed her graduate degree.

Two months later an economic catastrophe struck. On October 29, 1929, the stock market crashed. Millions of Americans lost their jobs, and the world went into a depression that lasted over ten years, until World War II.

Rachel's family was especially hard hit. Her parents had always struggled with financial problems and could no longer keep up the farm.

To help out, Rachel rented a house in Baltimore so her parents could live with her. Her divorced sister, Marian, and two little nieces, Marjorie and Virginia, moved in too. So did her brother. It was a very full house!

Maria handled the household chores while Rachel went to school and worked. In the evening, Rachel sat in front of the fireplace and read aloud to her nieces, just as Maria had done when Rachel was a little girl.

Rachel loved her family. However, she felt the constant stress of supporting them. In order to earn enough money, she cut back her classes and worked as a lab assistant and summer school teacher. Times were hard, but Rachel held on to her dream of becoming a marine biologist. In 1932 she successfully graduated with a master's degree in zoology.

She continued teaching, but there was never enough money. Her sister was in and out the hospital many times, and in 1935 Rachel's father died. Rachel needed a better-paying job, so she decided to contact Elmer Higgins once again.

Mr. Higgins was in the midst of a crisis when she arrived. He was trying to produce a series of radio programs about marine life, but not one of the biologists on his staff could write a decent script. When Rachel told him she could write, he hired her on the spot. Her talent as a writer made the scripts not only informational, but also very entertaining. The series was a huge success.

With Mr. Higgins' support and encouragement, Rachel took a government exam and became the first woman scientist at the agency. Her job was to write and edit pamphlets about sea life. Her two passions, science and writing, had come together! She later said, "It dawned on me that by becoming a biologist, I had given myself something to write about."

Rachel's appealing, easy-to-understand writing style taught Americans about nature and the importance of conservation. One of her favorite projects was writing a series of booklets about the national wildlife refuge system. Whenever possible she would pack up her binoculars, hand lens, and notebook, and explore a refuge in person. She wrote:

> Wild creatures, like men, must have a place to live. As civilization creates cities, builds highways, and drains marshes, it takes away, little by little, the land that is suitable for wildlife . . . Refuges resist this trend by saving some areas from encroachment, and by preserving in them, or restoring where necessary, the conditions that wild things need in order to live.

After working all day at the Fish and Wildlife Service, she often worked late into the night writing articles for magazines and newspapers. In 1937 Rachel submitted one of her articles to *Atlantic Monthly*, the top literary magazine in the country. The public loved Rachel's writing, and a publisher asked her to turn the article into a book.

However, Rachel's sister had died earlier in the year, leaving Rachel and Maria to take care of Marjorie and Virginia, who were eleven and twelve years old. With her full-time job and added family responsibilities, Rachel had little time for writing a book. It took her four years to complete *Under the Sea Wind*.

She wanted her readers to love the sea as much as she did. She also wanted them to understand ecology, the concept that everything is connected. She accomplished both of these goals by weaving scientific facts into an interesting story.

Her main characters weren't people, they were sea creatures—Silverbar, a seagull, Scomber, a mackerel, and a myriad of other animals. They described their life-and-death struggles under the sea in thrilling detail. At the same time they taught readers about the interconnectedness of life.

Unfortunately, Rachel's book was published in 1941, just as the United States was entering World War II. Despite fabulous reviews, book sales were terrible.

Undeterred, Rachel started research for a second book, *The Sea Around Us*. Published in 1951, the timing of this book was perfect. The war was over and people enthusiastically read Rachel's interesting and uplifting book. It skyrocketed to number one on the *New York Times* "Best Sellers" list, and stayed on the list for over a year and a half. The book's success launched Rachel as a celebrity. People wanted more, so *Under the Sea Wind* was re-published. This time, it became a bestseller too!

Book sales and speaking engagements meant that for the first time in her life Rachel didn't have to worry about money. She resigned as editor-in-chief at the Fish and Wildlife Service and fulfilled her life-long dream to live at the ocean. She built a small cottage on the Maine coast for herself, her mother, her niece Marjorie, and her niece's young son, Roger. Finally having some leisure time to spend with friends and family, she walked along the rocky shoreline, watched birds, and examined tide pools.

One rainy night Rachel wrapped little Roger in a blanket and carried him down to the beach during a fierce storm. Big waves boomed, throwing frothy spray into their faces. In a magazine article Rachel wrote, "Together we laughed for joy . . . I think we felt the same spine-tingling response to the vast, roaring ocean and the wild night around us." Ten years later her article was published as the book *A Sense of Wonder*.

With the ocean at her doorstep, Rachel was inspired to write her next book, *The Edge of the Sea*. Like the others, it became a bestseller. One review stated, "Miss Carson's pen is as poetic as ever and the knowledge she imparts is profound."

In 1956, Carson family history tragically seemed to repeat itself. Marjorie died. Just as Marjorie had been left an orphan in 1937, she left five-year-old Roger an orphan. And once again Rachel came to her family's aid. She adopted Roger as her own son, and helped him deal with the

Rachel and her niece, Marjorie, explore Maine's coast.

grief of losing his mother. Meanwhile she also cared for Maria, who was sick and elderly.

With so many family responsibilities, the last thing Rachel wanted to take on was another big book project. But a letter she received in 1958 from a friend changed her mind. It described how dozens of robins were killed when DDT was sprayed in the trees where they nested. "All of these birds died horribly . . . Their bills were gaping open, and their splayed claws were drawn up to their breasts in agony."

Rachel had been worried about DDT since 1945. Although the chemical manufacturers called it a "magic" cure against pests, Rachel had read research studies about the ways chemical pesticides poisoned the environment. She desperately wanted the public to know this information and asked several scientists to write about it. Each one refused.

Rachel could not remain silent. She decided she had to inform people herself. She spent four years researching and writing the book she would call *Silent Spring*. She carefully gathered data from experts in the scientific community, including her friend and famous ocean pioneer, William Beebe (see *Earth Heroes: Champions of the Ocean*).

While working on the book, Rachel suffered from many debilitating illnesses, including breast cancer. For several months during 1960, she couldn't walk or see properly due to radiation treatments. But Rachel kept working the best she could. Using enormous will power, she completed *Silent Spring* in 1962.

The book described the delicate balance between all of the Earth's systems—water, soil, air, and organisms. And it explained the ways chemical poisons upset that balance and kill life. Rachel documented the long-lasting effects of toxic chemicals and explained how DDT moved up the food chain to humans. Even human mother's milk contained DDT! The book also pointed out how alternative methods of pest control were cheaper, safer, and longer lasting than pesticides.

Although the chemical companies viciously attacked Rachel and *Silent Spring*, she had accomplished her goal. She had warned the public.

And once alerted, the public demanded action. President John F. Kennedy set up a committee to study pesticides. Congress passed new environmental laws and created the Environmental Protection Agency (EPA) to safeguard the health of people and the environment. A new generation of environmentalists was inspired by Rachel's ideas.

Ultimately recognized as an environmental hero, Rachel received many awards for *Silent Spring*. Sadly, she was often too sick and weak to attend the ceremonies in her honor. She died from breast cancer in 1964. After her death, a national wildlife refuge was named for her along the Maine coast that she so dearly loved. She was also posthumously awarded the Presidential Medal of Freedom, the highest honor a U.S. civilian can receive.

Although DDT was finally banned in the United States in 1970, vast amounts of chemicals continue to be poured into the environment, making the message of *Silent Spring* as relevant today as it was in the 1960s:

- Live in harmony with nature.
- Preserve and learn from natural places.
- Minimize the impact of man-made chemicals on natural systems of the world.
- Consider the impact of human activities on the global web of life.

FAST FACTS

Born: May 27, 1907, Springdale, Pennsylvania
Died: April 14, 1962, Silver Springs, Maryland
Children: Roger, her grandnephew and adopted son

ACCOMPLISHMENTS:
- Considered to be one of the most influential individuals the environmental movement
- Became the first woman biologist at the Bureau of Fisheries (now the U.S. Fish and Wildlife Service) and rose to a position of editor-in-chief
- Alerted the world to the dangers of indiscriminate use of pesticides, especially DDT
- Wrote four best-selling books and numerous environmental articles
- Inspired the creation of the Environmental Protection Agency (EPA) and numerous environmental laws
- Helped prevent the extinction of bald eagles, peregrine falcons, and other birds
- Financially and emotionally supported her parents, sister, niece, and grandnephew
- Received the Presidential Medal of Freedom

RIPPLES OF INFLUENCE:

Famous People Who Influenced Rachel Carson
Mary Skinker, Ernest Thompson Seton, President Theodore Roosevelt, Henry Williamson, William Beebe. Rachel was also greatly influenced by her mother, Maria.

Famous People Influenced by Rachel Carson
President John Kennedy, David Suzuki, Edward O. Wilson, Roger Tory Peterson, R.D. Lawrence

TIMELINE

Rachel Carson's Life		Historical Context
	1905	Audubon Society formed
Born May 27th	1907	
	1908	Roger Tory Peterson born
	1917	US enters WWI
Publishes first story in magazine	1918	
	1921	R.D. Lawrence born
Attends PA College for Women	1925	
	1927	
	1928	
Spends summer at Woods Hole, MA	1929	Stock market crash; E.O. Wilson born
	1930	Worldwide depression begins
Earns M.A. in marine zoology	1932	
	1933	Oria Douglas-Hamilton born
	1934	Jane Goodall born
Begins writing radio scripts	1935	
First government woman biologist	1936	
Atlantic Monthly article; sister dies	1937	William Hornaday dies
	1940	
Publishes *Under the Sea Wind*	1941	US enters WWII
	1942	Iain Douglas-Hamilton born
Becomes editor-in-chief for USFWS	1949	First UN conference on the environment
Publishes *The Sea Around Us*	1951	
Publishes *The Edge of the Sea*	1955	
Adopts Roger	1957	USSR launches first satellite, Sputnik
Begins writing *Silent Spring*; mother dies	1958	
Begins cancer treatments	1960	
Publishes *Silent Spring*	1962	Ding Darling dies
Dies April 14th	1964	
Rachel Carson NWR established	1970	EPA created; Saba D-Hamilton born
	1972	DDT banned in US
Awarded Pres. Medal of Freedom	1980	

54 Earth Heroes: Champions of Wild Animals

Roger Tory Peterson
1908–1996

The World's Foremost Birder

"We are beginning to understand the natural world and gaining a reverence for life—all life."

Making his way through the woods, eleven-year-old Roger noticed a pile of brown feathers huddled against the trunk of a tree just a few feet off the ground. What was it? A bird with its head tucked under its wings! The bird was motionless. Probably dead, Roger thought. Entranced, he stared at the bird for several moments, admiring its beautiful plumage. Then he reached out to touch its back with his finger.

Whoosh! Instantly the bird jerked its head around and exploded into flight. Roger saw a flash of gold under its wings and a red crescent on its neck as it disappeared into the woods. A flicker! The first one he had ever touched! Years later, he still vividly remembered the stunning sight:

> I can see it now—the way it was transformed from what we thought was death into intense life. I was tremendously excited with the feeling, which I have carried ever since . . . It was the contrast, you see, between something I thought was dead and something so alive. Like a resurrection. I came to believe birds are the most vivid reflection of life. It made me aware of the world in which we live.

This 1919 experience was one of the major turning points in Roger Tory Peterson's life.

Roger's interest in birds was nurtured by his seventh-grade teacher, Blanche Hornbeck, who started a Junior Audubon Club after school. She wasn't a bird expert, but she had a desire to learn about them, and she invited her students to join her. Club membership cost ten cents.

Roger was one of the club's most enthusiastic members. He treasured the packet that arrived each month from the National Association of Audubon Societies. It contained a four-page leaflet of bird information, a bird portrait by a well-known artist, and a line drawing of a bird to color.

At one of the club meetings Miss Hornbeck gave Roger a small box of watercolors and a drawing of a blue jay to paint. Blue jays were one of his favorite birds, and he eagerly set to work copying the details from a colored illustration in a reference book. Roger was very proud of the way he "carefully painted the jay's blue feathers highlighted with white and black, its jaunty crest, and downy-gray breast."

From that moment on, painting birds became his lifelong passion, and Roger Tory Peterson earned a worldwide reputation as one of the most influential bird illustrators in history.

About the time that Roger was getting interested in birds, he read the book *Two Little Savages* by Ernest Thompson Seton. Seton, who also coauthored the first Boy Scout manual, explained many scouting skills through the storyline of the book. The main character, Yan, and his friend learned how to live in nature "like Indians," using plants and animals for food and shelter.

Roger identified whole-heartedly with the fictional Yan. Both Roger and Yan were Swedish, both loved being outside in nature, and both wanted to run away and be free. Neither of them did well in school, and neither of them had fathers who understood them. Yan had his friend, Sam; Roger had his real-life friend, Clarence Beal. Roger and Clarence imitated the adventures described in the book as they slept outside in lean-tos, caught crabs and boiled them in big tin cans to eat, and learned about every aspect of nature.

In the chapter "How Yan Knew the Ducks from Afar," Seton, through his character Yan, explained a major problem with bird field guides. Their drawings showed how the ducks looked if they were close up, as if being held in a person's hands. But Yan never got an up-close look at a duck. He only saw them from a distance. Then Yan noticed that all ducks had slightly different feather patterns, which he called their "uniforms." These patterns were like identification tags.

Yan made drawings to show how each duck's unique feather pattern looked from a distance. Using these drawings as a guide, Yan could quickly identify ducks at a glance. *Two Little Savages* included two pages of these "far-sketches."

The sketches had a huge impact on Roger. He wished that there was a guide that depicted all birds as simply as the ducks in Seton's book. But none existed.

When Roger went bird watching, he tried to notice one or two visual cues for each of the birds he saw. Remembering these cues, he was quickly able to identify many birds. This technique became the basis for the "Peterson System" of bird identification.

Roger and Clarence were true nature companions. They spent many hours exploring the local woods, fields, and lakes. One spring day they took a train to Lake Erie, listing all the different kinds of birds they saw and heard along the way. Their grand total was 123. Roger was extremely competitive when it came to listing birds. He always wanted to see more birds than Clarence and be the first one to identify a new species. His determination to be the best stayed with Roger all of his life.

Birds fascinated Roger. He was obsessed with learning everything he could about them. He hauled books home from the library in his red wagon, pulling it one and a half miles uphill. He began reading magazines written by *ornithologists*, scientists who study birds. He also read *Bird-Lore*, now called *Audubon* magazine, and *National Geographic* magazine. Little did he realize that one day he would be writing articles for both of these well-known publications.

Inspired by the book *Wild Wings*, written by the adventurer Herbert K. Job, Roger decided to "hunt" birds with a camera rather than a gun. This was a new way of observing birds in the 1920s. At that time, naturalists shot birds so they could closely study them. Even the famous John James Audubon killed birds in order to paint them accurately for his book, *Birds of North America*.

Through photography, Roger knew he could study birds without killing them. He saved up his money to buy an Eastman Primo Number 9, the first of many cameras he would own. On winter mornings, Roger and Clarence would put seed and suet at various bird feeding stations they had set up on the outskirts of Jamestown. In the afternoon they would return to take photos of the nuthatches, chickadees, and other birds that came to the feeders.

While in high school, Roger's interests expanded to include butterflies and moths, catching them in a net his mother made for him. Not only did he collect mature butterflies, he also gathered caterpillars before they turned into butterflies. One year he discovered some rare pipevine swallowtail caterpillars—800 of them! He kept them in jars all over the house and fed them leaves until they went into their chrysalis stage. Roger risked angering his neighbors as he raided gardens to pick enough pipevine leaves to keep the caterpillars alive.

Roger collected butterflies during the day and moths at night. The moths were attracted to the streetlights late at night, but nighttime collecting posed a problem. Jamestown, New York, had a curfew. All children had to be off the streets by 8:45 p.m. However, Roger used his ingenuity to figure out a solution. With great self-confidence he walked into city hall and explained the predicament to the police chief. Fortunately, the chief was sympathetic and created a special permit for him. It read: "This permits Roger Peterson to catch moths around streetlights until 11 p.m."

Roger's mother was extremely tolerant of his unusual collections. She didn't object when he attached dozens of moth cocoons to the living room curtains. However, his father and sister were irate when heat from the coal stove caused the moths to emerge in the middle of winter. The moths flew around the house laying sticky white strings of eggs everywhere.

The family living room was also the location of Roger's flower collection. During what he called a "botanical big day," Roger and Clarence collected 220 flowering plants. Roger brought the flowers home and pressed them under the carpet between sheets of newspaper. As with birds, Roger's early interest in flowers was expressed years later when he illustrated *A Field Guide to Wildflowers* in 1968.

Roger felt perfectly at home in nature. But in school he was a misfit. He was the youngest and smallest boy in the class when he started high school at the age of twelve. He wasn't good at sports, and most of his classmates thought he was odd because he spent so much time watching birds and tramping around in the woods. They teased him, calling him "the kook" and "Professor Nutty Peterson."

In looking back on his school experience, Roger described himself as "the school nonconformist." He was proud that he was an individualist, doing things he enjoyed no matter what others thought of him.

Art was Roger's favorite subject. He decorated the margins of his school papers with illustrations of birds, butterflies, and wildflowers, just as he had seen on the pages of *Two Little Savages*. The back of his science lab notebook contained a drawing he labeled "trade mark"— a

After graduating from high school, Roger used his artistic skills to make a living by painting furniture.

pair of binoculars and a butterfly net next to a butterfly and a robin.

Despite his lack of interest in most school subjects, Roger graduated when he was sixteen. Underneath his graduation picture in his 1925 high school yearbook it read: "Woods! Birds! Flowers! Here are the makings of a great naturalist." How true that turned out to be.

After graduation, Roger would have liked to roam the woods all day, but his father demanded that he go to work. Fortunately, Roger found a job that used his artistic talent—painting delicate designs on expensive Chinese-style cabinets at a furniture company.

He saved up enough money from his job to travel to a meeting of the American Ornithologists' Union (AOU) in New York City. This trip was one of the most memorable events of Roger's life because it gave him the opportunity to meet many of his heroes in the world of birds. The highlight was meeting Louis Agassiz Fuertes, a famous bird artist whom Roger idolized. It was Fuertes' painting of a blue jay that Roger had first copied when he was in the Junior Audubon Club!

Fuertes was kind to Roger and generously spent time with him. Together they viewed the AOU art exhibit where two of Roger's paintings were displayed. As they parted, Fuertes reached into his coat pocket and pulled out one of his paintbrushes—a present for Roger. What a treasure!

Fuertes also opened a door of opportunity to Roger by saying, "Don't hesitate to send me your drawings from time to time." Roger, just seventeen years old, was overwhelmed by this offer from such a distinguished painter to critique his work. Not wanting to waste Fuertes' time, Roger kept waiting until he had a painting that he considered "worthy" before sending him something. Unfortunately, Fuertes was killed in an accident less than two years later. Roger lamented, "And so, by delaying, I forfeited a priceless opportunity."

After the AOU meeting, Roger considered two possible careers. He could go to college at Cornell University and become an ornithologist, or he could go to art school and have a career as a painter. His father didn't like either choice. He thought Roger should keep working at the furniture company in Jamestown.

As it turned out, Roger's finances made the decision for him. He just didn't have enough money to go to college. Instead, he worked in Jamestown for two more years. But by 1927 he had saved enough to return to New York City and enroll in art school. He supported himself by painting furniture.

Roger commented years later that he probably never would have created his unique system of bird identification if he had gone to college. Because of his art background, he approached birds visually rather than scientifically. As a result, the Peterson Identification System was born.

New York City might seem like an unlikely place for bird watching, but Roger discovered the Bronx County Bird Club—a group of young men who were as enthusiastic about birding as he was. They traveled all over the area going to wildlife refuges, parks, bays, and even to garbage dumps to identify birds. Their mentor, Ludlow Griscom, was considered one of the premier bird watchers in the country. He held club members to the highest standard of accuracy.

The camaraderie with like-minded friends and the competition to see the most birds were pure joy for Roger. It was with these friends that he developed and perfected his identification skills. Reflecting on that time in his life, Roger said that if it had not been for the influence of the Bronx County Bird Club, "I would have devoted my life to painting.

Birding would have been a hobby." Fortunately for millions of bird watchers, birding became his primary focus.

During the summer break from art school in 1928, Roger took a job as a counselor at Camp Chewonki, a boys' camp on the coast of Maine. There, Roger's natural teaching ability blossomed under the guidance of Clarence Allen, the camp's director. Roger would take the boys exploring in the woods, learning as they went. He took risks that he probably shouldn't have, such as chasing moose, climbing tall trees, and canoeing in five-foot waves. The boys absolutely loved it!

Allen described Roger this way: "He was able to impart enthusiasm and excitement to his young camp friends. Roger led the boys up hills and over gullies, going up trees and up to [their] middle in swamps . . . They soon discovered that every foot of the way revealed something new." For five years, Roger spent his summers at Camp Chewonki and his winters in art school in New York City.

In December 1930, he was on a birding excursion with his friend William Vogt, a nature columnist. Vogt was amazed at how quickly and accurately Roger could identify birds after only a quick glimpse. While searching for eagles and canvasback ducks, Roger showed Vogt some of the sketches he used for identification. They were simplified drawings, similar to the ones Roger had seen in *Two Little Savages*. Roger had also added small arrows pointing to each bird's most important field marks.

Vogt said, "Roger, you know more about identifying the birds of this region than almost anyone else. And you can paint. Why don't you pass on your knowledge to other people in a book?" As they walked back to their car, Roger and Vogt developed the plan for Roger's field guide. It was another important turning point in Roger's life.

However, getting an idea for a book and actually writing it are two different things. The book was a huge undertaking. Roger had to find a way to support himself while he wrote it. But he couldn't find a job. The country was in the midst of the Great Depression.

Allen again came to Roger's aid. In addition to directing Camp Chewonki, Allen was also the headmaster of Rivers School, a prestigious private school in Brookline, just outside of Boston, Massachusetts. He offered Roger a job as a natural history and art teacher.

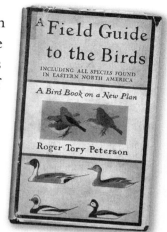

As a teacher, Roger had a special way of inspiring his students. Expressing his own genuine interest and enthusiasm, Roger was like a "Pied Piper" as he led students on field trips into nature. And he also brought nature into the classroom. Mrs. Allen commented, "Roger would bring a bird in, set it down on the desk, and talk about it to the boys. And the bird wouldn't mind!" The boys would just sit there with their mouths open, enthralled.

Roger taught during the day and wrote at night. Although his knowledge of birds was immense, he painstakingly researched the 425 birds included in the book using four main sources: museums, living birds, ornithology books, and scientists. He studied specimen skins and drew on the expertise of his experienced bird-watching friends. His 500 illustrations were researched just as thoroughly as his descriptions.

The result was a user-friendly field guide, simply titled *A Field Guide to the Birds*. Roger kept the guide small enough to carry along into the field. His descriptions were short and interesting, making the reader feel as if Roger were a companion along on the trip. His illustrations were simple, with obvious field marks indicated by one or two arrows. The book made birding easy for a beginner, yet contained enough information to satisfy the advanced birder.

Published in 1934, the *Guide* became an instant success. The first printing of two thousand copies sold out within the first week! Positive reviews poured in from well-respected ornithologists as well as amateur bird watchers. At the age of twenty-six, Roger had initiated a worldwide

Roger's bird paintings were accurate and simple. His identification system influenced millions of Americans.

change in the way people saw and identified birds, which influenced the way people related to the environment as a whole.

Over the course of his lifetime, Roger revised the book five times, redoing most of his illustrations and many of the descriptions. He also wrote three editions of *A Field Guide for Western Birds*. His bird field guides have sold over seven million copies.

Roger's identification system was adapted to other aspects of nature. Over fifty books now make up the *Peterson Field Guide Series*, including guides for wildflowers, reptiles, insects, rocks, fish, mushrooms, and even the stars. Through his field guides, Roger made the natural world accessible to millions of people around the world.

E. O. Wilson, the acclaimed author-scientist, expressed immense admiration for Roger. He called him a true scientist who made major contributions to the field of ornithology. In 1988, in *The Birder's Handbook*, Paul Ehrlich wrote:

In this century no one has done more to promote an interest in living creatures than Roger Tory Peterson, the inventor of the modern field guide. His greatest contribution to the preservation of biological diversity has been in getting tens of millions of people outdoors with Peterson field guides in their pockets.

Soon after the *Guide* was published, Roger went to work at the National Association of Audubon Societies. His life had come full circle. As Audubon's education director, he revised the Audubon leaflets—the same leaflets that introduced him to birds in seventh grade!

Combining his talents for writing and painting with his skills as a teacher, Roger shared nature information in a way that appealed to children. Roger's Audubon leaflets reached over nine million children and their parents. A former president of the National Audubon Society, Carl Buchheister, said, "Roger's leaflets were more important in educating people about birds than his field guides."

A blend of hard work, talent, and mentoring brought Roger to a point of success. The devotion and support of his second wife, Barbara, helped his success continue. She managed their home and raised their two sons, Tory and Lee, which gave Roger the freedom to focus on his work. Barbara also played a key role as Roger's business manager. She booked his speaking engagements, answered his letters, arranged his travel schedule, and typed his manuscripts. Later in life, Roger's third wife, Virginia, supported him in similar ways.

Roger's success with the *Guide* opened many doors. He became a celebrity, traveling the world from Africa to Antarctica, from the Gobi Desert to the Galapagos Islands. Every place he went, he described, painted, and photographed birds.

His birding skills were exceptional and sometimes highly unusual. During one birding trip, he surprised his companions by lying on the ground and closing his eyes. Everyone thought he was taking a nap. After several minutes, Roger stood up and identified over twenty species of birds just by listening to their chips and chirps.

Roger loved birds. Birds loved Roger!

Roger's magnetic personality and enthusiasm for nature attracted many interesting friends, including Lars-Eric Lindblad, a modern-day explorer. Lindblad took him to Antarctica where Roger got his first sight of penguins. He was immediately captivated! When asked to choose a bird nickname Roger said, "I decided on King Penguin, my favorite species in my favorite family of birds."

One of Roger's closest friends was the English naturalist James Fisher. Both expert birders, they broke the world record by identifying 600 birds during their 30,000-mile trip around the shoreline of North America. *Wild America*, the book about their 100-day journey, became another one of Roger's bestsellers.

Current birding experts, including David Sibley and Kenn Kaufman, trace their interest in birds to Roger. Kenn says, "Getting started as a crazed little-kid birder . . . I read and virtually memorized all of his books and magazine articles I could find."

The words "ecology" and "environmentalism" are now common, but Roger was ahead of his time in 1951 when he described nature's interconnectedness. From his book *Wildlife in Color*:

> Our world is "one world," where everything is interdependent—
> soil, robins, and hickory trees, brook trout, damselflies, and mink—
> and men.

He recognized the dangers of DDT in 1957 when he noticed a decline in the number of osprey eggs in the nests he monitored near his

Connecticut home. Roger said, "Birds are indicators of the environment. If they are in trouble, we know we'll soon be in trouble." Five years later his friend Rachel Carson published *Silent Spring*.

Roger expressed environmental principles through his writings. But he didn't want people just to read about nature. He wanted them to experience an emotional connection with nature. He believed that their connection would inspire them to learn more. And once they had a greater understanding, they would begin to care for the environment.

His writing, especially his field guides, helped people feel confident that they could go outside and experience nature directly. Today, the Roger Tory Peterson Institute of Natural History in Jamestown, New York, supports Roger's environmental ideals. The Institute offers exhibitions, programs, and special events that encourage an increased awareness and appreciation of the natural world.

Roger died in 1996 at the age of eighty-seven. During his life he received every major award in the field of conservation, and over two dozen honorary degrees. When President Carter awarded Roger the Presidential Medal of Freedom, the nation's highest civilian honor, he said, "He has impassioned thousands of Americans, and has awakened in millions across this land, a fondness for nature's other two-legged creatures."

Roger himself described his accomplishments in simple terms: "My main contribution has been along the lines of putting things in people's hands so they could learn of the natural world."

FAST FACTS

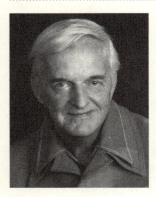

Born: August 28, 1908, Jamestown, New York
Died: July 28, 1996, Old Lyme, Connecticut
Wives: Mildred Washington, Barbara Coulter, Virginia Westervelt
Children: Tory and Lee

ACCOMPLISHMENTS:
- Developed the "Peterson System" of field identification
- Wrote or edited over 50 field guides including *A Field Guide to the Birds*
- Wrote numerous books including *Wild America*, *The Bird Watcher's Anthology*, *The Junior Book of Birds*, *Birds Over America*, and *How to Know the Birds*
- Contributed articles, artwork, and photographs to magazines including *Life*, *Bird-Lore*, *Audubon*, *The Bird Watcher's Digest*, and publications of the World Wildlife Fund and the National and International Wildlife Federations
- Received the Presidential Medal of Freedom and many other honors.

RIPPLES OF INFLUENCE:

Famous People Who Influenced Roger Tory Peterson
John James Audubon, Louis Agassiz Fuertes, Ernest Thompson Seton, Ludlow Griscom, Frank Chapman, Arthur A. Allen, James Fisher, Peter Scott, Keith Shackleton, Lars Lindblad, and Blanche Hornbeck

Famous People Influenced by Roger Tory Peterson
Elliot Richardson, Rachel Carson, E.O. Wilson, Paul Ehrlich, Thomas Lovejoy, David Allen Sibley, Peter Alden, Pete Dunne, Victor Emmanuel, Kenn Kaufman

TIMELINE

Roger Tory Peterson's Life		Historical Context
	1905	Audubon Society formed
	1907	Rachel Carson born
Born August 28	1908	First Ford Model T car produced
Touches first flicker	1919	Theodore Roosevelt dies
	1921	R. D. Lawrence born
Graduates; attends AOU meeting	1925	
Begins art classes in New York	1927	First talking movie released
Goes birding with Bronx Co. Bird Club	1928	
	1929	Stock market crash; E.O. Wilson born
Works at Camp Chewonki in Maine	1930	Worldwide depression begins
Begins *Guide*; teaches at Rivers School	1931	
	1933	Oria Douglas-Hamilton born
A Field Guide to the Birds is published	1934	Jane Goodall born; 1st Duck Stamp
Marries Mildred Washington	1936	David Suzuki born
	1937	William Hornaday dies
Paints birds for *Life* magazine and *NWF*	1939	WWII begins in Europe
	1942	Iain Douglas-Hamilton born
Marries Barbara Coulter	1943	
Begins *Peterson Field Guide Series*	1947	
Travels around No. America with Fisher	1953	DNA discovered
	1962	*Silent Spring* published; Darling dies
Testifies to Congress about DDT	1964	
	1970	Saba Douglas-Hamilton born
Makes film *Wild Africa*	1972	U. S. government bans DDT
	1973	Endangered Species Act is passed
Marries Virginia Westervelt	1976	
Receives Pres. Medal of Freedom	1980	Voyager I reaches Saturn
	1989	Large oil spill occurs in Alaska
Establishes Roger T. Peterson Institute	1993	
Dies July 28	1996	Ebay website created for online auctions
Latest edition of *Guide* is published	2008	

Ronald "RD" Lawrence

1921–2003

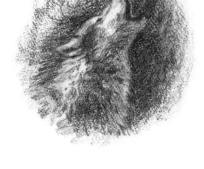

Friend of the Wolf

"There are no villains or heroes in the forest, for every creature has its own part to play."

The trees hid the pack of wolves from view, but Ron knew they were tightening their circle around him. *Howl-bark! Howl-bark! Howl-bark!* Closer and closer they came. Grabbing an ax in one hand and a long pole in the other, he scrambled to the top of a nearby log pile, hoping the height would give him a fighting advantage.

Ron caught glimpses of the wolves as they moved among the trees. They were big! Time stopped as Ron, gripped with fear, waited for them to make their move.

He knew that fear was normal. He had experienced it many times during the war. But if he gave in to his fear, there was a good chance he would die. Taking control of himself, Ron decided to act.

"*Yaahh!*" he yelled as he leapt from the log pile. Continuing to shout, he waved his ax and club aggressively as he strode through the trees towards the trail. The howls of the wolves were all around him, but Ron forced himself to ignore the threats as he pushed through knee-deep snow. Although his progress was slow and clumsy, his adrenaline-charged body kept propelling him forward.

It took him almost an hour to reach his closest neighbor. Ron borrowed a rifle and made his way back to the logging site. He was determined to take revenge on the wolves that had scared him so badly.

His senses were on high alert as he approached the log pile. His rifle was at the ready to shoot the first wolf he saw. He later recalled, "But apart from the chirping of chickadees and sound of wind stroking the tree tops, all was quiet."

Ron relaxed somewhat and carefully surveyed the scene. Wolf tracks led him into nearby trees where he found the scattered remains of a deer on the bloodstained snow.

Like a detective who has gathered all the clues to solve a mystery, he gradually realized what had *really* happened. His arrival at the logging site had disturbed the wolves while they were eating their kill. As Ron later described, "The pack had bluffed me with their howl-barking and circling, and, when I left the area, they returned to their meal and finished it in peace."

Ron was amazed that the wolves hadn't killed him. They could easily have done so. Instead, they had simply and deliberately just frightened him off. He marveled at their intelligent, effective strategy.

This first encounter with wolves was a major turning point for Ron. He was "filled with the desire to study those hauntingly fascinating animals . . ." The experience also reawakened his longtime interest in studying *all* aspects of the natural world—an interest he had neglected for several years.

Ron's earliest memory of being enthralled with wildlife happened in 1926. He was just four years old, living with his family in a Spanish fishing village on the Mediterranean Sea. One afternoon, while momentarily unsupervised, he wandered down to the beach and walked right into the salty sea water. Without fear, he kept his eyes opened wide as the warm water washed over his head. All at once he was captivated by the sea life he saw beneath his feet.

After that marvelous experience, his parents couldn't keep him out of the water. In their attempt to ensure his safety, they made him wear a life belt so he would at least float on top of the waves. But Ron wanted to dive down to the sandy bottom to see the fish and crabs more closely, and the belt prevented him from doing that. Every day he would swim out to a rock outcropping away from his parents' view and secretly take off the belt. He was usually caught and scolded, but he just kept doing it. Finally his father relented and gave him permission to swim without the belt, much to his mother's dismay.

He learned his first marine biology lessons from the marine creatures themselves. A prickly sea urchin taught him about animal defenses as two of its barbs painfully pierced his finger. When his legs became tangled up in seaweed, he learned to avoid thick patches of kelp. And one nip from a crab was enough to teach him how to pick one up without getting his fingers pinched.

He discovered that sea creatures died quickly if put in jars, so he created natural "aquariums" in tide pools near the shore. Scrounging food from a local fisherman, he was able to keep his fish and crabs alive and healthy.

Early mishaps and adventures taught Ron to have lots of patience. He learned to respect each plant and animal and get to know it. When he made a new discovery, he controlled his enthusiasm and just looked at the specimen for a while, rather than recklessly grabbing at it. This practice of careful observation stayed with him his entire life and gave him the opportunity to have incredible experiences with wildlife.

On his fifth birthday, Ron received a fishing rod and reel and a new scoop net. He immediately set out to use them. But catching his first fish turned out to be a traumatic experience. As he tried to remove the hook, he ripped the fish's lower lip. His father told him to throw the fish against a rock to kill it. But Ron absolutely refused! Instead, he put it safely

into a nearby tide pool so he could care for it.

In 1933, at the age of eleven, Ron spent the summer with his aunt on the Spanish island of Majorca in the Mediterranean. While exploring a kelp bed off the rocky coast, he noticed something swimming among the fronds. It was a young shark! In fact, there were several of them, each about twelve inches long. They were the first he had ever encountered.

He caught, observed, and studied the sharks throughout that summer and during the next two summers as well. Ron learned a lot about shark behavior and noticed that once he understood

Ron didn't know he would grow up to become an author, but he learned to type when he was only seven years old.

why sharks behaved as they did, his fear disappeared. As an adult, he applied this same lesson to wolves.

When he wasn't swimming in the ocean, Ron explored the forest behind his aunt's villa. On one of his excursions he met an elderly Czechoslovakian gentleman who had been a botany professor at Prague University. Ron had difficulty pronouncing the man's name, so he simply called him "the Professor."

They established a routine that suited both of them quite well. Ron spent his mornings swimming in the ocean, tending to his captured sharks, fish, and crabs. Then he spent his afternoons studying with the Professor. In his autobiography, Ron wrote:

Patient, calm, and infinitely devoted to his specialty, the old gentleman turned the forest into an absorbing classroom, teaching me more during our time together than I was to learn about botany at school during all the years I attended classes.

The Professor explained that all living things in the forest were connected. Ron was puzzled. Although most people today understand "ecology," at that time it was a new concept to science. Ron asked if he meant that "a flower was connected to a tree and a beetle connected to the flower." The professor beamed at him and spoke words that Ron remembered for the rest of his life: "Exactly so. *All is one.*"

In describing his childhood, Ron called himself "a happy loner engrossed in the natural world." He wrote, "I cannot recall a single day when I was bored."

His happiness came to an abrupt end on July 18, 1936, with the beginning of the Spanish Civil War. His mother was Spanish, but his father was English, so arrangements were made for him to go immediately to the English Consulate. From there he would catch a ship to England. But Ron had his own ideas. Lying about his age, the fourteen-year-old boy told the authorities he was sixteen and joined the government militia.

The harsh realty of war hit him immediately. During his first night as a soldier, he killed a man in order to save himself. When he turned around, his best friend lay dead next to him. That was just the beginning of many bloody battles that Ron would fight for the next three years.

After the civil war ended, he lived in peace for only a few short months before World War II broke out in Europe. As a British citizen, Ron immediately enlisted and became a gunner on a tank. Death and destruction filled his life for another five years. In 1944, on the beaches of Normandy, his tank was shelled, killing Ron's entire crew. Miraculously, he survived. But he was severely injured.

Ron was flown to a hospital in England to have his leg amputated. But he just couldn't imagine life with only one leg and convinced the doctor to try to save it. Fortunately, the doctor was able to remove all but two of the thirty-nine pieces of shrapnel in Ron's leg without amputating it.

When the doctor informed him that he would always walk with a limp, Ron totally dismissed the idea. Calling forth all his will power, Ron exercised every day despite the pain. He promised himself he would walk properly in a year or less. It was a promise he kept!

Due to his injuries, Ron was "invalided out" of the service. For the next seven years, he attended Cambridge University, worked as a journalist, got married, and had a son. Although many people would like such a settled life, Ron wasn't happy. Restless and bored, he sailed to Canada in 1954 to start a new life for himself and his family at the age of thirty-three.

Even though the temperature was four degrees below zero F when he arrived, Ron felt a kinship with the Canadian wilderness and the people who lived there. He bought a small homestead in Ontario's backcountry and set to work cutting logs for a mill. That's when his first encounter with wolves reignited his interest in studying the natural world.

Combining his naturalist, scientific, and writing skills, he began keeping detailed journals of his encounters with wolves and other animals, including lynx, moose, bear, hares, and the various birds at his homestead. He continued this practice everywhere he lived in Canada. His journals later became the basis for many of his award-winning

Earth Heroes: Champions of Wild Animals

nature books, including *The Zoo That Never Was*, *Secret Go the Wolves*, and *Ghost Walker*.

Ron was content living a life of hard work and nature study. But his wife wasn't. She went back to England with their two children. Ron's only companions were his dogs, but they were more than enough for him.

Susie, a collie-husky mix, first came to him on a winter evening while he sat comfortably next to the stove reading his book by lamplight. He heard a scratching at the door, and when he opened it, the dog just walked right in. She sat down, "smiled" at Ron, and swished her tail back and forth as if to announce, "I'm home." Ron thought Susie would make a good sled dog, so he bought two more dogs, Rocky and Sooner.

His fourth dog, the leader for his dog-sled team, arrived one day when his friend Charley pulled up at Ron's homestead in an old pickup truck. The animal in the back was three-quarters dog and one-quarter wolf. Ron described his first look at the wolf-dog this way: "Chained to a ring at the cab end of the truck box stood the largest, most evil-looking dog I had ever seen. As I approached the vehicle, the monster peeled back his lips, opened his mouth . . . and delivered a deep snarl . . ."

At first, Ron didn't want to have anything to do with this savage creature, but then the wolf-dog's yellow eyes bored into his. There was something in them that deeply touched Ron. In that moment he decided to keep him. He gave him a wilderness name: Yukon.

Yukon and Ron bonded deeply and quickly. Ron wrote, "Three days later, Yukon had become my close companion. In fact, he was already teaching me how to love, an emotion I later realized I had never before experienced."

Ron came to understand the depth of that love one night when he and Yukon discovered a bear behind the house. Not even a full-blooded timber wolf is a match for a bear. Nevertheless, Yukon chased the bear into the forest. Ron stumbled through the trees, calling him. But Yukon was gone. Ron searched for him all night. When he found a patch of ground covered in blood, he knew there had been a terrible fight. Ron returned home exhausted and depressed.

Sitting alone in his living room thinking about Yukon, Ron's heart broke open. He realized that years of war, suffering, and death had taken their toll. As a defense, he had closed himself off from all others. He didn't love anyone or anything. And that's the way he liked it. But living in the wilderness had helped heal his emotions. When Yukon finally returned two days later, Ron was a changed person. He treated Yukon's many wounds, and their bond was stronger than ever.

About this same time, another change came into Ron's life. He could no longer ignore how brutal it was to trap animals. In a moment of truth, he threw all of his traps into a deep lake. However, the money he had been earning by selling fur pelts was an important source of income. Ron couldn't afford to stay on the homestead without that money.

To solve his dilemma, Ron left his homestead to live a life in the wilderness. He and Yukon headed west, camping, fishing, and hunting along the way. For the little money he needed, Ron wrote articles for various newspapers and wire services. They traveled across Canada for fourteen months, having exciting adventures in Manitoba, Saskatchewan, and British Columbia.

During their wilderness adventures, Yukon taught Ron a lot about wolf behavior. Yukon demonstrated a wolf's extraordinary senses when he guided Ron through a blizzard. Yukon showed a wolf's strength and bravery when he saved Ron from a charging bull moose. And when Yukon sniffed out another wolf's hidden den of pups, he led Ron there, giving Ron a glimpse into a wolf's family life.

Yukon eventually mated with a wild wolf and left Ron. Although Ron was happy that Yukon was living a life of freedom in the wilderness, he missed him. Fortunately, many more wolves came to him throughout the rest of his life.

Two special wolves were Matta and Wa. Ron rescued them while on a backcountry canoe trip in 1968. Wet and bloody, they were wrapped in their mother's hide. She had been killed for the meager $25 bounty the Canadian government paid for killing wolves. Just a week old, the pups were completely helpless and on the brink of death.

Having spent over ten years raising various animals, Ron prided himself on being able to feed and care for all kinds of babies, from baby mice to moose calves and even bear cubs. His only problem with these pups was that he didn't have his usual assortment of bottles and nipples. They were back at his farm, many miles away.

He solved the problem in an unusual and creative way—he filled his mouth with formula and stuck out his tongue. The wolf pups learned by trial and error to drink the milk that trickled down Ron's tongue.

Ron and his second wife, Joan, added these wolves to the menagerie of orphaned and abandoned animals that lived with them on their Ontario wilderness farm. Matta and Wa thrived; and like so many of the animals Ron rehabilitated, they returned to the wild "healthy, strong, and free."

Ron rehabilitated wolves and many other wild animals, including this red-tailed hawk.

Ron raised the wolves in secret. He had to hide them from his neighbors who would have killed them. They thought the same way many people still do, that wolves are dangerous to humans and wildlife. At one time, killing wolves was an accepted practice, and wolves were exterminated from most of the United States and many parts of Canada by 1930.

Ron knew better. He had studied the vital role wolves played in the northern forest ecosystem and wrote, "There are no villains or heroes in the forest, for every creature has its own part to play . . . Each is ensuring the continuation of nature, for in the wilderness death is a part of life." Through decades of observation of both wild and captive wolves, Ron concluded that wolves and the wolf pack are the "ultimate stabilizers" of an environment.

Biologists eventually realized the truth of Ron's words. Where wolves had been killed off, the plants and other animals suffered dramatically. Rivers and streams eroded. Fish, frogs, beavers, and turtles disappeared. And deer and elk overgrazed young trees, stopping new growth in the forest.

Wolves were completely wiped out in Yellowstone National Park in 1926, but were reintroduced in 1995. As Ron had done years earlier, scientists began observing the key role wolves play in keeping a balance in nature. *The Planet in Peril,* a CNN documentary, reported, "Having more wolves has helped rebalance the park's ecosystem. Gray wolves hunt the large animals like elk that were eating so many plants that some of the [plants] were in danger of disappearing."

The results in Yellowstone and other study areas prove that the health of an entire ecosystem relies on the presence of the top predators in that ecosystem's food chain. Top predators vary by habitat and include not only wolves, but also animals such as bear, pumas (also called mountain lions and cougars), and sharks.

The concept that *death sustains life* is a common theme in the more than thirty books Ron wrote using his initials R.D. Lawrence. Considered a "storyteller for animals," Ron portrayed each species he wrote about "as it really was." His captivating stories, based on his personal experiences with animals, emphasize that life and death are *both* important parts of the same cycle.

Ron faced the sorrow of death in his own life in 1969, when Joan died unexpectedly. Once again he turned to the solitude of nature for comfort. Sailing along the rugged coast of western Canada for one and half years, he weathered fierce storms and swam with blue sharks and orcas.

When he returned to Ontario, Ron married Sharon Frise, and together they started rehabilitating sick, injured, and abused animals. Hundreds of people visited them each year at their 100-acre home and wildlife reserve in Ontario's Haliburton Highlands. Ron shared his understanding of wildlife, writing books and articles, lecturing, and supervising graduate students.

Sharon notes, "Ron mentored hundreds of young people . . . so they in turn could continue to educate and influence younger generations." In that way Ron passed on the inspiration he received from *Earth Heroes: Champions of the Wilderness* hero Henry David Thoreau. "Perhaps the greatest influence in my life, and writings, comes from Thoreau,"

Ron said in an interview. "At fourteen I read *Walden* and was deeply impressed by one of Thoreau's sentences: 'In wildness is the preservation of the world.'"

Ron supported "wildness" in all forms, but especially in wolves. One of his most significant contributions was helping to establish the Haliburton Forest and Wildlife Reserve Wolf Centre in Ontario. A gray wolf pack was brought to the Centre from northern Michigan, and in 1994 the first litter of pups was born. Today, more than 30,000 guests a year visit the wolves at the Centre, learning about them and their habitat. The Centre also conducts wolf research.

Without Ron's efforts, Canada's only wolf center would not exist. He made frequent appearances as wolf expert and presenter at the Centre and shared his advice on an ongoing basis.

Ron with Tundra, a wolf he and his wife Sharon rehabilitated.

Ron died in 2003, but people continue to be influenced by his insights into animal behavior and the wolf myths he dispelled.

MYTH	FACT
Wolves are vicious killers and attack people, as depicted in stories such as *Little Red Riding Hood* and *The Three Little Pigs*.	Wolves kill to eat and survive. In all of North America, there are very few documented cases of a healthy, wild wolf attacking people.
Wolves kill large numbers of livestock, such as sheep and cows.	Livestock losses caused by wolves are minuscule compared to those caused by weather, disease, and other predators.
Wolves will kill off entire wildlife game populations.	As proven in Yellowstone, wolves help maintain a balanced ecosystem, including sustainable wildlife populations.

Ron believed that wolves are a much closer model of human behavior than primates. He thought we could learn a lot about ourselves by understanding them. A true friend of the wolf, four years after his death he was recognized with a Lifetime Achievement Award by the International Fund for Animal Welfare for his "passion, dedication and commitment to animals and the natural environment."

FAST FACTS

Born: September 12, 1921, aboard a ship in the Bay of Biscay near Spain

Died: November 27, 2003, Ontario, Canada

Wives: Shirley, Joan Gray, Sharon Frise

Children: Simon and Alison

ACCOMPLISHMENTS:

- Journalist and newspaper editor worldwide
- A storyteller for wild animals, writing more than 30 books, including award-winning *North Runner* and *Ghost Walker*
- Received several awards for conservation writing
- Awarded the "Commemorative Medal of Canada"
- Helped establish Haliburton Forest and Wildlife Reserve Wolf Centre
- Saved countless injured and orphaned animals, large and small
- Posthumously awarded the IFAW "Lifetime Achievement Award"

RIPPLES OF INFLUENCE:

People Who Influenced R.D. Lawrence
Henry David Thoreau, Ralph Waldo Emerson, John Muir, Jack London, John Steinbeck, E.O. Mitchell, Rachel Carson, Jane Goodall, Richard Leaky, Charles Darwin, Kalahari Bushmen, Douglas Pimlott, Aldo Leopold, Adolph Murie, Al Gore, Thor Heyerdahl, Jacques Cousteau

People Influenced by R.D. Lawrence
Influenced thousands through his writings and personally mentored hundreds of young people

TIMELINE

R.D. Lawrence's Life		Historical Context
Born September 12	1921	
Discovers marine life for the first time	1926	Last wolf killed in Yellowstone NP
	1929	Stock market crash; E.O. Wilson born
Explores marine life on Majorca	1931	
	1933	Oria Douglas-Hamilton born
Studies with the "Professor"	1934	Jane Goodall is born
Joins militia in Spanish Civil War	1936	Spanish Civil War begins
	1937	William Hornaday dies
	1938	Spanish Civil War ends
Joins British Army to fight in WW II	1939	World War II begins
	1942	Iain Douglas-Hamilton born
Severely injured; has leg operation	1944	D-Day in Normandy
	1945	World War II ends
Marries Shirley	1950	
Moves to Canada and buys homestead	1954	
	1957	USSR launches 1st satellite, Sputnik
Explores wilderness with Yukon	1958	
Meets Joan and marries her 2 years later	1960	
	1962	Carson writes *Silent Spring*; Darling dies
Writes 1st book, *Wildlife in Canada*	1966	
Rescues wolf pups Matta and Wa	1968	
Joan dies at the age of 33	1969	
	1970	Saba Douglas-Hamilton born
Sails along coast of British Columbia	1972	U. S. government bans DDT
Marries Sharon Frise	1973	Endangered Species Act is passed
Focuses on animal rescue in Ontario	1984	
	1995	Wolves reintroduced to Yellowstone
Haliburton Wolf Centre opens	1996	
Finishes last book, four in progress	1997	
Dies November 27	2003	US begins war in Iraq

Earth Heroes: Champions of Wild Animals

Edward O. Wilson

1929—present

Lord of the Ants

"If insects were to vanish, the environment would collapse into chaos."

Paradise Beach on Florida's Gulf Coast was a great place for a little boy. The fish were biting and seven-year-old Edward Wilson sat on the dock, happily catching one pinfish after another. Baiting his hook with a minnow, he dropped it into the water and waited for the telltale tug. He felt it! Quickly he yanked the fish out of the water. But he pulled too hard. Ouch! As the fish smacked him in the face, one of its sharp spines pierced his right eye.

The pain was excruciating. Ed suffered for hours, but didn't tell anyone because he wanted to keep fishing. It wasn't until several months later, after Ed was back home in Alabama, that his parents noticed that something was wrong. Ed was blind in his right eye. Fortunately his left eye had excellent short-range vision. However, this childhood accident in 1936 played a significant role in determining the course of Ed's life and his career as a naturalist.

The following January, Ed experienced another traumatic event—his parents divorced. They sent Ed to the Gulf Coast Military Academy in Mississippi for the rest of the school year while they rearranged their lives.

The Academy was like a boot camp for boys. The rules and regulations were strict, and for the first few days he was confused and lonely. Although he soon adapted to the rigid daily schedule, he yearned for the freedom to wander at the beach fishing and exploring. Nevertheless, many of the lessons and values he learned at the Academy stayed with him throughout his life, including self-discipline, responsibility, appreciation for hard work, and devotion to duty.

In 1938 Ed went to live with his father and stepmother. The family constantly moved from town to town. Over an eleven-year period, Ed attended fourteen different schools. He was always the "new kid." Instead of trying to make a lot of friends, he spent his time alone in the woods, fields, and marshes. Nature became his "sanctuary and a realm of boundless adventures."

When he was nine, Ed moved to Washington, D.C. For him it was a "magic kingdom" highlighted by two treasures, the National Museum of Natural History and the National Zoo. Both places were free of charge and open to the public every day.

He spent every spare moment exploring the museum, carefully studying the exhibits and displays. He pulled out the display drawers of butterflies and other insects, while envisioning the far-off places where these creatures had lived. For the first time he became aware of the profession of museum *curator*—a person who has expert knowledge about plants and animals and shares their expertise with the public. He imagined how wonderful it would be to spend his whole life learning about plants and animals.

Next to the zoo was Rock Creek Park, a natural oasis in the middle of the city. Ed and his newfound friend, Ellis MacLeod, went on insect-collecting expeditions in the shady woods along the creek. Making their own butterfly nets out of broomsticks, coat hangers, and cheesecloth, they caught many different butterflies, including such beauties as red admirals and great spangled fritillaries.

One day, as Ed scrambled up a steep hill, he stopped to peel the bark off a rotting tree stump. Underneath he discovered a seething mass of ants that quickly vanished into the heartwood of the stump. Just then, Ed noticed a distinctive lemony scent. With that clue, he was able to identify them as citronella ants. Thirty years later in his research lab he learned how these and other ants use scent to communicate.

Both Ellis and Ed decided to become *entomologists*—scientists who study insects. Insects were an excellent choice for a budding naturalist like Ed whose eyesight and hearing weren't very good. Reflecting on this decision Ed wrote: "I turned my attention to the little things of the world, the animals that can be picked up between thumb and forefinger and brought close for inspection."

When Ed moved to Mobile two years later, he completely immersed himself in Alabama's natural world. His parents gave him "indirect support" by simply allowing him the freedom to go exploring on his own. Passionate about butterflies, he imagined he was a big-game hunter with a net as he set out to capture rare specimens. He also "hunted" small reptiles, stunning them with his slingshot so he could take them home for his collection. His stepmother was tolerant of his specimens until one day he came home with a brown snake wrapped around his neck. She ordered him to take it as far away from the house as possible!

During his excursions, Ed learned all he could about Alabama's plants and animals. Sometimes these lessons were painful, like the time he mistakenly used the stems of poison oak to build a secret outdoor shelter. He developed a severe and painful rash over a large part of his body. And when he pretended to be a South American explorer chopping his

At thirteen, Ed caught insects with a homemade net next to his family home in Mobile.

way through the undergrowth, he accidentally slashed his finger to the bone with a machete. He left a trail of blood as he rode his bike home. He realized that in some situations he needed to be more careful. However, it took a few more painful lessons before he learned to be careful around snakes.

When Ed was thirteen, his friend Ellis came to spend the summer with him. Their adventures together rekindled Ed's desire to become an entomologist. He decided to study and collect all of the various species of ants in a vacant lot next to his house in Mobile. Identifying them by their scientific names (genus and species), he found two types of ants common to Alabama: trap-jawed ants, *Odontomachus insularis*, and small yellowish-brown ants, probably *Pheidole floridana*.

He also made a major scientific observation: a colony of imported fire ants, *Solenopsis invicta*. These ants were native to South America and no one had ever seen them in the United States. Ed was the first person to record their presence! Fire ants became one of his favorite species to study; and fifteen years later, when he was at Harvard University, he used them to make an important scientific breakthrough.

While living in Mobile, Ed became what he called a "child workaholic," delivering 420 newspapers every day before school. Each morning he got up at 3:00 a.m. and made two trips to the delivery dock to pick up all of his newspapers. His head was barely visible above the stacks of papers strapped to his bike. It took him four and a half hours to complete his route, which gave him just enough time to grab breakfast and rush off to school. Saturday afternoons were his only free time, his time to escape into nature.

Ed didn't complain about working so hard. The money he earned allowed him to participate in one of his favorite activities—scouting! In his autobiography, *Naturalist*, Ed wrote, "The Boy Scouts of America seemed invented just for me."

Everything about scouting—the uniforms, oath, and motto— appealed to him. The scout values of hard work and pursuit of honorable goals reinforced his military school training. Scouts gave him something he wasn't getting in school: the opportunity to challenge himself, learn at his own pace, and advance to a level of excellence.

In just three years he achieved the highest rank—Eagle Scout with palm clusters. Along the way he earned forty-six merit badges. The scouting program also gave Ed, a self-described "undersized introvert," a comfortable way to make friends and an opportunity for leadership.

At the age of fourteen, he was the youngest nature counselor at scout camp and figured out a foolproof plan to get his campers interested in natural history. Snakes! Although most of the boys were afraid of snakes, they were fascinated by them. Whenever they spotted one, the call would go out, "Snake! Snake!" Ed, the brave and respected snake authority, would capture it and tell the boys all about the species. He soon filled a row of cages with snake specimens and became both the "zoo director" and tour leader. He was also the "natural history instructor," giving lectures about the snakes and the diversity of plants and animals in that region of Alabama.

As an adult Ed reflected, "The Boy Scouts of America seemed invented just for me."

The zoo's star attraction was a cage of pygmy rattlesnakes. Although not as deadly as diamondback or canebrake rattlesnakes, their bite was poisonous and somewhat dangerous. Ed became prideful and rather careless around them. One day, while cleaning the rattlesnake cage, he moved his hand too close to a coiled snake. With surprising speed, the snake sprung forward and sunk its fangs into the tip of Ed's finger.

Ed endured a painful operation to remove as much of the venom as possible, and then recuperated at home while the swelling in his arm subsided. When he returned to camp, the cage of pygmy rattlers was gone, and he was forbidden to touch any more poisonous species. He obeyed this order while at camp, but his fascination with poisonous snakes stayed with him.

In 1944 his family moved to Florida's panhandle, one of the best areas in the world for snakes—over forty different species! With such diversity, Ed's interest in reptiles and amphibians intensified. He bicycled to a fish hatchery located next to a dense swamp on the edge of town at every opportunity. Donning high wading boots, he explored the mysteries of the wet, green world. He wrote:

> The hours I spent there were among the happiest of my life . . . In the swamp I was a wanderer in a miniature wilderness. I never encountered another person there, never heard a distant voice, or automobile, or airplane . . . the terrain and its treasures belonged entirely to me in every sense that mattered.

Ed searched for and captured lots of different snakes, keeping them in homemade cages at his house. Some of his favorites were the eastern ribbon snakes that draped themselves over tree branches. The most dangerous snakes in the swamp were the poisonous cottonmouth water moccasins. Peterson's *A Field Guide to Reptiles and Amphibians of Eastern and Central North America* declared: "Don't ever handle a live one!"

Ignoring the warning, Ed caught many young cottonmouths, some up to eighteen inches long. But one day he tangled with an enormous adult that might have easily killed him. At five feet long, it was the largest cottonmouth he had ever seen. The snake's body was as big around as his arm, with a head the size of his fist. Ed was thrilled! He wanted it for his collection.

He moved into the shallows and grasped the snake behind its head. As he lifted it out of the water, it responded violently. Twisting and

Poisonous snakes didn't scare Ed, until one day he wrestled a giant cottonmouth water moccasin.

turning its powerful body, the snake stretched its head toward Ed's hand. Its opened mouth revealed two-inch fangs. Ed struggled, knowing he was about to lose control. Finally, using all of his strength, he "heaved the giant out into the brush, and it thrashed frantically away." What a close call! As the adrenaline surged through his body, he knew he had been lucky.

Ed's snake hunting explorations in the swamp were reckless, but also exhilarating. He was sorry to leave the magic of his swamp paradise when his family moved once again—this time to central Alabama.

In 1945, at sixteen, Ed decided that it was time to get serious about his career as an entomologist. He wanted to focus on a single species of insect so he could become a world authority on it. At first he chose the fly.

But he ran into a problem when he tried to buy long insect pins, an essential piece of equipment for a fly collection. The pins were made in Czechoslovakia, which was a war zone. No pins were available. Ed wasted no time in selecting another insect. Returning to his previous passion, he decided he would become a *myrmecologist*—an entomologist who specializes in the study of ants.

The next hurdle Ed had to face was figuring out a way to pay for a college education. The solution seemed to be to get government financial assistance by enlisting in the Army. However, to Ed's great disappointment, he failed the Army physical examination because he was blind in one eye. His childhood accident with the pinfish continued to influence his life.

But Ed refused to give up his dream! Standing on the steps of an Army administration building, he wiped the tears from his eyes and vowed that nothing would keep him from his goals. He swore he would graduate from college and become an important scientist.

That's just what he did. Fortunately, the University of Alabama had lower fees than other schools, and his father and mother were able to provide the money he needed. He worked hard to graduate in three years, which also kept his costs down. Afterwards, he earned an M.S. from Alabama and a Ph.D. from Harvard University.

During college, Ed continued doing what he loved to do as a little boy—discover and learn about new species of ants. When he was only a sophomore, the Alabama Department of Conservation asked him to conduct an environmental study on fire ants, the species he had discovered as a thirteen-year-old. He took four months off from school and traveled all over Alabama conducting experiments and observations.

He published his first scientific article documenting the spread of fire ants and explaining the crop damage they caused.

His talent, hard work, and accomplishments earned him a reputation as a promising scientist. At Harvard he was selected to become a member of the Society of Fellows—a high honor. As a junior fellow he had the opportunity to do research on islands of the South Pacific. Having always loved the tropics, Ed was thrilled to go to such an ideal location. It was unexplored territory, and he would be the first pioneer collecting ants!

Although he was excited to pursue his professional dreams, he was also reluctant to leave. He had fallen in love with Renee Kelly, and it was terribly hard to say goodbye to her. During the ten months he was away, they wrote over six hundred letters to each other! They married when he returned in 1955.

Ed described the South Pacific as a "galaxy of thousands of islands." While exploring the island of New Caledonia, he felt the same sense of personal adventure that he had felt in the swamps of Alabama. Everything he saw, every plant and animal, was new to him.

He followed the advice he had received earlier from Philip Darlington, an accomplished entomologist. He said, "Ed, don't stay on the trails when you collect insects. Most people take it too easy when they go into the field ... You should walk in a straight line. Try to go over any barrier you meet. It's hard, but it's the best way to collect."

Ed didn't take the easy route. His greatest physical adventure came when he journeyed into the interior of New Guinea. After slogging through the dripping rainforest and climbing slippery mountain slopes, he became the first biologist to reach the highest peak of the Sarawaget mountain range. At the summit he looked down on a natural scene that may have appeared the same as it had 100 million years earlier. He wrote, "I had reached the edge of the world . . . and knew myself better as a result."

It took Ed several years to analyze and catalog the hundreds of specimens he had collected on his trip. Then, following his curiosity, he began researching ant communication. To observe the behavior of an entire colony of fire ants easily, he constructed a plexiglass nest.

Through experiment and observation he discovered that "ant language" consists of chemicals that ants release from their bodies. These chemicals are called *pheromones*. Ants taste and smell pheromones to "talk" to one another. For example, when a scout ant finds a source of food, she lays down an invisible chemical trail by touching the bottom of her abdomen to the ground. Other ants follow the trail to find the food. Ed estimates that ant vocabularies vary between ten to twenty different signals. In addition to a signal for "food," they also have signals for "danger" and "move to a new nest site."

One of Ed's favorite pheromone discoveries was finding out how ants chemically determine that one of them is dead. He said, "It's not enough for the ant to be lying still with his legs sticking up in the air. It has to have a certain decomposition substance that it only gets after a couple of days. That substance is oleic acid." Ed discovered that when he dropped oleic acid on a perfectly healthy ant, the other ants treated it as if it was dead. They picked it up and dumped it on the garbage pile! The ant then had to completely clean itself off before it was considered "alive" and allowed to rejoin the colony.

Ed's discovery with ant communication was a major scientific breakthrough because many animals do most of their "talking" through chemical pheromones. By the 1960s many other scientists had followed his footsteps into pheromone research. Always a pioneer, Ed decided to explore new areas of ant study.

He conducted experiments and made discoveries about the social aspects of ant colonies. Working with his friend and colleague Bert Hölldobler, he wrote four books. Their first book, *The Ants*, won a Pulitzer Prize in 1990. Their third book, *The Superorganism: The Beauty, Elegance, and Strangeness of Insect Societies* (2009), explains how a colony of millions of ants acts like a single, giant organism. An entire chapter is devoted to leafcutter ants.

> Leafcutters are gardeners, growing white fungus farms on the leaves they harvest. It can take more than a million ants to support the queen, and every member of the colony has a job to do. Some harvest the leaves, some tend the 'garden' and others protect it from invaders.

Ed also wrote a book about the most abundant group of ants in the Western Hemisphere—*Pheidole*. Of the 624 known species in this group, Ed has discovered 341 of them. He also meticulously drew all five thousand illustrations for the book.

Although Ed is considered *the* world authority on ants, he is also an original and creative thinker in many other areas. Where most people see separate subjects, Ed sees relationships. He has the ability to study the details of the tiniest ant and at the same time keep in mind the big picture of the whole environment. He's made important discoveries about life on islands, as well as the connection between genetics and behavior in all animals. He also introduced the new concept of *biophilia*, suggesting why humans have a natural love for other living things.

Biodiversity refers to all life in an ecosystem. Ed was the first person to outline its principles and practical aspects. He explained that biodiversity is essential for our survival because it provides important medicines for healthcare; materials for industry; and critical ecosystem services, including air purification, clean water, flood control, and fertile soil.

Ed warns that humans are changing or destroying Earth's environment. As species become extinct, the planet loses its diversity of life. But he says it's not too late. Although humans can destroy the planet, they can also protect it.

To highlight biodiversity, Ed and wildlife expert Peter Alden created the world's first Biodiversity Day in 1997 at Thoreau's famous Walden Pond. People came together to list all of the plants and animals they could find around the pond. The event was so successful it led to a statewide program. During an eleven-year period, the citizens of Massachusetts recorded almost 150,000 species of plants and animals in their state.

BioBlitzes grew out of Biodiversity Day 1997 and are held in many communities worldwide. Children and adults work alongside professional naturalists, wildlife managers, and research scientists to observe and record as many native plants, animals, and fungi as possible. The results help scientists learn about the biodiversity of an area.

Another way that Ed has inspired awareness of biodiversity is through the online *Encyclopedia of Life*. This encyclopedia lists and explains every species of life on the Earth. The pages are created collaboratively by both professional scientists and amateurs. It is freely available to everyone at www.eol.org.

Ed's life has been devoted to discovery. He says:

> It's always been a dream of mine, of exploring the living world, of classifying all the species and finding out what makes up the biosphere. But we have only identified about 10% of the life on earth. Ninety percent of the species of organisms on Earth are still undiscovered. We live on an unexplored planet.

Many of the organisms that are yet to be discovered are invisible to the eye. Even though they are microscopic, they are crucial to life on Earth. In 2009 Ed told an audience that included many students, "If you really want to discover something new and have a great future in science, study bacteria, fungi, slime molds, or viruses."

Ed has had many role models throughout his life. The people he finds easiest to admire are "those who concentrate all the courage and self-discipline they possess toward a single worthy goal: explorers, mountain climbers, ultra-marathoners, military heroes, and a very few scientists. Science is modern civilization's highest achievement, but it has few heroes."

Interested in the world's tiniest creatures, Ed carefully observes the minute details of an ant.

For many people, Ed Wilson is one of these heroes—a scientist who has dedicated his life to teaching others about life on earth. His ideas have influenced the ecology movement and conservation decisions worldwide. He has won over one hundred major awards, and both *TIME* and *Audubon* magazines have recognized him as one of the century's 100 leading environmentalists. Ed encourages young people with this advice:

> You are capable of more than you know. Choose a goal that seems right for you and strive to be the best, however hard the path. Aim high. Behave honorably. Prepare to be alone at times, and to endure failure. Persist! The world needs all you can give.

FAST FACTS

Born: June 10, 1929, Birmingham, Alabama
Wife: Renee Kelley
Daughter: Catherine

ACCOMPLISHMENTS:
- Attained highest rank of Eagle Scout
- Discovered the first fire ant colony in the United States
- Discovered 341 new species of the ant genus *Pheidole*
- Recognized as the world's leading authority on ants
- Discovered how ants use pheromones to communicate
- Wrote over 20 books; awarded two Pulitzer Prizes
- Pioneer in the field of biogeography
- First to outline and explain the principles of biodiversity
- Explained new concepts: sociobiology and biophilia
- Influenced the growth of ecology
- Considered a "founding father" of the environmental movement
- Promoted the *Encyclopedia of Life*

RIPPLES OF INFLUENCE:

Famous People Who Influenced E. O. Wilson
Charles Darwin, William Beebe, Sir Arthur Conan Doyle, Philip Darlington, many colleagues including Robert MacArthur and Bert Hölldobler

Famous People Influenced by E. O. Wilson
David Attenborough, many colleagues including Robert MacArthur and Bert Hölldobler. He has also influenced thousands of students.

TIMELINE

E. O. Wilson's Life		Historical Context
Born June 10	1929	Stock market crash
	1933	Oria Douglas-Hamilton born
	1934	First Duck Stamp; Jane Goodall born
Fishing accident; loses eyesight	1936	National Wildlife Federation formed
Parents divorce; attends military school	1937	William Hornaday dies
Explores museum & zoo in Wash., D.C.	1938	
	1939	WW II begins in Europe
Discovers 1st fire ant colony in US	1942	Iain Douglas-Hamilton born
Struggles with large cottonmouth	1944	
Earns Eagle Scout's highest rank; Chooses to study ants as a career	1945	World War II ends
	1949	First UN conference on environment
Leaves for South Pacific islands	1954	
Marries Renee Kelley	1955	
Becomes professor at Harvard	1956	
	1962	Carson writes *Silent Spring*; Darling dies
Selected for Nat'l Academy of Sciences	1969	
	1970	Saba Douglas-Hamilton born
Made Curator of Entomology, Harvard	1972	U. S. government bans DDT
	1973	Endangered Species Act passed
Publishes *Sociobiology*	1975	
Receives the National Medal of Science	1977	
Wins Pulitzer Prize for *On Human Nature*	1979	Three Mile Island meltdown
Publishes *Biophilia*	1984	
	1988	NASA scientist warns of global warming
Wins Pulitzer Prize for *The Ants*	1991	
Publishes *Diversity of Life*	1992	Earth Summit held in Rio de Janeiro
Time's 25 Most Influential People	1995	
	1997	First BioBlitz held
Proposes an *Encyclopedia of Life*	2003	US begins war in Iraq
	2006	*An Inconvenient Truth* released
	2008	*Encyclopedia of Life* debuts on Internet
Writes *The Superorganism*	2009	

Edward O. Wilson

Earth Heroes: Champions of Wild Animals

Jane Goodall
1934—present

Ambassador for Wild Chimps

*"Only if we understand, can we care;
Only if we care, will we help;
Only if we help, shall all be saved."*

Jane was scrambling through the rainforest's wet undergrowth when a dark shape in the tall grass caught her attention. Peering through her binoculars she saw a male chimpanzee squatting on the earthen mound of a termite nest. She recognized the chimp as "David Greybeard," a name she had given him because of the white hair on his chin.

Giving names to animals was a very *unscientific* thing to do. But Jane wasn't trained as a scientist. She hadn't even gone to college. However, she was a keen observer of animal behavior. And what she observed David Greybeard doing on that African afternoon in 1960 sent shockwaves through the scientific community and made her famous around the world.

As Jane intently watched, the chimp picked a wide blade of grass and pushed it into the termite nest. After a few moments, he carefully pulled it out and put it up to his lips. He repeated this action again and again, every so often using a new piece of grass. When he left, Jane went to the nest and imitated his behavior. As she pulled out her own blade of grass, she saw that it was covered with termites.

At that moment she had a startling realization. David Greybeard had used a piece of grass as a "fishing pole" to "fish" for termites! This was a monumental discovery. It was the first time an animal had been observed using a tool, in this case a piece of grass. Until then, people believed that only humans used tools. A few days later Jane saw another

Young Jane with "Julbilee," her favorite toy.

chimp strip leaves off a twig and use the bare twig to fish for termites. Another major discovery! Chimpanzees not only *used* tools, they actually *made* them!

Jane continued to study the chimps, unaware of the turmoil caused by her discoveries. Scientists were in an uproar. If animals used tools, they would have to change their definition of what it meant to be human. And many of them refused to do that. Some said that Jane's observations couldn't be trusted because she was so young, just twenty-six years old. And she didn't have any scientific credentials. Others suggested that she *taught* the chimps to use grass and twigs! Now, after decades of observations, scientists know that chimpanzees use many types of tools. For example, they use leaves as sponges and rocks as hammers.

Fortunately, the National Geographic Society recognized the importance of Jane's discovery and gave her grant money to continue her work. Over the years they also published many magazine articles and made documentaries about Jane and her life with chimpanzees.

Living with wild animals in Africa was the fulfillment of Jane's lifelong dream. A seed for that dream was planted in 1936, when she was only eighteen months old. At that time, Jane's family was living in London and a baby chimpanzee was born at the London Zoo. To honor the special event, Jane's father gave her a life-like chimpanzee stuffed animal named Jubilee. Family friends warned Jane's parents that the toy would give Jane nightmares. But she loved it! She recalls, "Jubilee instantly became my most cherished possession and accompanied me on nearly all of my early childhood adventures."

At age four, Jane did her first "serious" animal field study while visiting her paternal grandmother's farm. She was puzzled about how an egg could come out of a chicken because she didn't see an opening big enough. So she crawled into the hen house and waited.

> It was very stuffy and hot where I crouched, and the straw tickled my legs. There was hardly any light either. But I could see the bird on her nest of straw . . . If I moved I would spoil everything. So I stayed quite still. So did the chicken. Presently . . . I saw a round white object gradually protruding from the feathers between her legs. It got bigger. Suddenly she gave a little wiggle and —plop!—it landed on the straw.

Meanwhile, the entire household was frantically looking for her. At 7:00 p.m. she finally appeared. Jane had been missing for four hours! Her mother, Vanne, wrote, "There were little bits of straw in her hair and on her clothes, but her eyes, dark ringed with fatigue, were shining." Sensing Jane's excitement, Vanne didn't scold her. Instead she listened with full attention as Jane described the wonderful event she had just witnessed.

Jane now realizes how lucky she was to have such an understanding mother. Vanne lived to be ninety-four and supported Jane's love for animals and passion for knowledge throughout her long life. "Jane," Vanne said, "if you really want something, and if you work hard, take advantage of the opportunities, and never give up, you will somehow find a way." If it hadn't been for Vanne, Jane knows she might never have achieved her dream of living with wild chimpanzees in Africa.

The beginning of World War II in 1939 played an important role in Jane's life. Her father immediately joined the British Army. Jane, Vanne, and Jane's younger sister, Judy, all moved to her maternal grandmother's house in southern England. It was called The Birches.

Jane loved living at The Birches. It felt warm and comfortable. There was a big backyard (called a "garden" in England) with a green lawn, lots of trees, and many secret places where Jane imagined fairies and gnomes danced in the moonlight. "My love for nature grew as I watched birds making their nests, spiders carrying their egg sacs, squirrels chasing each other around the trees," she later wrote in her book, *Reason for Hope*.

One summer Jane organized a nature club, the Alligator Club, with her sister and two friends. The club set up "camp" in a hidden little clearing behind some bushes. Over a small fire, they boiled water for tea in a tin can balanced on rocks. Because food was rationed during the war, their "feasts" consisted of leftovers or a few crusts of bread, and sometimes a cookie. Jane remembers it as great fun, "especially when we crept out into the garden at midnight, which we did partly because it was spooky and partly because it was strictly not allowed!"

When Jane was about seven, Vanne brought *The Story of Dr. Doolittle* home from the library. Jane read it. Then read it again. The night before it was due to be returned, she read it yet again by flashlight under the bedcovers. Jane longed to talk to the animals like Dr. Doolittle. To her happy surprise, she received her very own copy of the book at Christmas.

The Jungle Book and *Tarzan* were two of Jane's other favorite books. She later wrote, "It was daydreaming about life in the forest with Tarzan that led to my determination to go to Africa, to live with animals, and write books about them."

Jane had lots of pets including cats, guinea pigs, and a canary. But her most beloved animal was a dog named Rusty. He was a mixed breed, all black except for a white patch of fur on his chest. Although Rusty belonged to Jane's neighbors, he and Jane were practically inseparable. As soon as his owners let him out in the morning, he came to The Birches and stayed with Jane until she went to bed.

Jane taught Rusty lots of tricks. Not only would he shake hands, roll over, and play dead, he would also climb ladders and jump through a hoop. Jane says that Rusty taught her about the *true* nature of animal behavior, lessons she later applied to her field studies with chimpanzees.

"Rusty the dog taught me that animals have personalities, minds, and feelings of their very own."

Jane also loved horses and spent most Saturdays at a riding stable. Vanne couldn't afford to pay for riding lessons, but Jane didn't care. She just liked being with the horses. She did chores around the barn and farm and, because she worked so hard and enthusiastically, was often rewarded with a free ride. Jane became an excellent rider, and when she was fourteen she had the thrill of riding a show pony and entering jumping competitions.

Jane was outside and in the garden as much as possible. She often did homework atop her favorite tree—a big beech tree she simply called Beech. She wrote, "I could feel a part of the life of the tree, swaying when the wind blew strongly, close to the rustling of the leaves . . . I could sometimes lay my cheek against the trunk and seem to feel the sap, the lifeblood of Beech, coursing below the rough bark."

As a teenager, Jane spent many happy hours working at a stable and participating in horse competitions.

She also went high into Beech's branches to think. The war, the atom bomb, and the Holocaust affected her deeply. Sitting high above the world, she tried to make sense of good and evil in the world.

At nineteen, Jane still dreamed of going to Africa to live with wild animals, but she had to be practical. Her family didn't have money to send her to college, and she needed a job. Vanne told her that she could find work anywhere in the world if she had secretarial skills, so Jane went to London to train to be a secretary.

She didn't really like her secretarial classes, but the city's museums, art galleries, and theaters delighted her. And she made lots of friends who opened her eyes to new ways of thinking about the world.

After graduating, Jane worked at various secretarial jobs, and then in 1956 an unexpected opportunity came along. One of her high school friends had moved to Africa, and she asked Jane to come for a visit. Jane was overjoyed! But first she had to earn enough money for the trip.

Jane moved back to The Birches and got a job as a waitress. The work was exhausting, but she kept focused on her goal. One night, after five months of working and saving every penny, she closed the living room curtains and counted her money. She had enough! She could make her dream come true.

Traveling first by boat and then by train, Jane arrived in Nairobi, Kenya, on April 3, 1957—her twenty-third birthday. On the way to her friend's farm, Jane saw her first giraffe up close. In her book *My Life with the Chimpanzees* she wrote:

> He stood on his long legs in the middle of the dirt road, his long neck towering above the car, and looked down his long nose at us. His beautiful dark eyes were fringed with long lashes... Finally he turned and cantered away. It looked as though he ran in slow motion. When I saw him, that amazing long animal, I finally knew, for sure, that I was really there. I had actually gotten to the Africa of my dreams—the Africa of Dr. Doolittle and Tarzan.

After a few wonderful weeks of visiting and sightseeing, Jane went back to Nairobi to work as a secretary. Vanne had been right. Having secretarial skills allowed her to work anywhere in the world.

Her interest in animals soon led her to the famous Louis Leakey, the man known for discovering important clues to human evolution. Leakey was both an *anthropologist*, a scientist who studies human culture and evolution, and an *archaeologist*, a scientist who studies prehistory by excavating sites and analyzing the artifacts. When Jane met him, Leakey was in charge of the Coryndon Museum, now called the National Museum.

She described her first impressions: "We met in his large, untidy office, strewn with piles of papers, fossil bones, and teeth, stone tools, and all sorts of other things." She considered him "a real genius with an inquiring mind, enormous energy, great vision, and a marvelous sense of humor." She had no idea, at that time, that he would make her dream of living with wild animals come true.

Not everyone was so appreciative of Leakey. Some scientists thought he was unorthodox and unprofessional. Most people agreed that he was very unusual. Nevertheless, Jane and Louis impressed each other, and he immediately offered her a job as his secretary. She happily accepted.

Before Jane began her work at the museum, Leakey and his wife, Mary, took her on a three-month expedition to dig fossils at Olduvai Gorge on the Serengeti Plain. This site is now world famous for the humanlike skull that was found there, but in 1957 Olduvai Gorge was completely unknown and very isolated.

Digging for fossils was hard work. The sun was hot and the days were long. But after the day's work, Jane had enough energy to go exploring. Once she was followed by a male lion; on another occasion she almost bumped into a black rhino. At night she listened to the "giggling" of hyenas. "I had never been so happy," she wrote. "There I was, far, far from any human dwellings, out in the wilds of Africa, with animals all around me in the night. Wild, free animals. That was what I had dreamed of all my life." Back in Nairobi, Jane took full advantage of working for Leakey at the museum. Everything interested her, and she learned all she could about African animals.

However, Jane didn't like being surrounded by dead animals. She wanted to be with *living* ones! Leakey gave her that chance when he asked her if she wanted to conduct a study of chimpanzees in the forested hills of Tanganyika (now called Tanzania).

Leakey had watched Jane carefully, and felt she had the qualities to be a successful field researcher. She was a hard worker, extremely patient, loved animals, and was very knowledgeable about them. She had proven she could live in primitive conditions. Most importantly, she had an open mind, uncluttered with scientific theories.

Not everyone agreed with Leakey. Some thought he was "out of his mind" to send an untrained girl into danger. But Leakey didn't listen to them. He knew Jane was the right person to conduct the study. It took him a year, but he finally was able to make all the necessary arrangements for her to study the chimps at the Gombe Stream Game Reserve (now Gombe National Park).

On July 14, 1960, Jane landed on the eastern shore of Lake Tanganyika. She thought it was paradise. Rain forest covered Gombe's steep hills and many streams ran into the lake. Jane's study area, approximately thirty square miles, included three lush valleys. In addition to chimpanzees, the reserve was home to baboons, red colobus and vervet monkeys, squirrels, mongooses, and many reptiles and birds.

Frustrating for Jane, her observations of chimpanzees didn't begin right away because they were afraid of her. Although she caught glimpses of them through her binoculars, they ran off whenever she approached. They moved freely through the trees, while she struggled through dense undergrowth trying to follow.

Her luck changed one morning when she climbed to a rocky outcropping about 1000 feet above the lake. Calling it "the Peak," Jane found it the perfect vantage point to spot chimps as they moved through the forest. She began most days at 5:30 a.m. climbing up the steep slope to the Peak in early morning darkness. Sometimes she even spent the night.

With patience and careful observation, she learned to distinguish individual chimps. Like all the animals she had ever known, Jane gave them names. David Greybeard was the first chimp to visit Jane's camp and take the banana she offered. He showed the others that Jane wasn't a threat, and she was soon able to observe the chimpanzees more closely.

Another one of Jane's favorite chimps was Flo, a female with a bulbous nose and ragged ears. Flo, with her daughter Fifi and son Fagan, taught Jane what it meant to be a chimp mother. Jane delighted in watching the antics of the young chimps and admired Flo's patience in teaching them.

Jane approached animal observation in her own unique way. Not only did she give the chimps names instead of numbers, she set up feeding stations and also made physical contact with some. She took her cues from the chimps and related to them personally, as she had done with Rusty and all of the animals she had known. Not everyone agreed with these methods, but despite criticism and controversy, Jane is now recognized as the world's foremost primatologist.

As early as 1963, articles and photographs of Jane and the chimps appeared in *National Geographic*. In 1965 the film "Miss Goodall and the Wild Chimpanzees" was shown on American television. Jane became a worldwide celebrity. As a spokesperson for chimps, she gave lectures, published articles, and wrote books. Gombe Stream Research Center was established in 1967, and Jane became the director, supervising graduate students and other researchers.

While Gombe was growing and changing, so was Jane's personal life. She earned a Ph.D. in ethology, the science of animal behavior; got married; and had a baby, nicknamed Grub. She was a dedicated mother, and the chimps influenced her to make time every day to play with Grub. To Jane's disappointment, her first marriage ended in divorce. She happily remarried in 1975, but sadly, her second husband died in 1980.

Fifty years after Jane began her study, the chimpanzees of Gombe are still being studied. It's the longest-running study of its kind in the world. In addition to the breakthrough discovery that chimps use tools, Jane and the Gombe researchers have made other significant observations, including:

- Chimps are not strictly vegetarians. They also eat meat, such as bush pigs. Two chimps became cannibalistic in 1975, eating the babies of other chimps.

- Diseases such as polio and pneumonia affect chimps.

- Chimps are capable of warfare. A large group of Gombe chimps waged a four-year "war" on a smaller group, systematically killing all of the males.

- Chimps have emotions. When they see friends they get excited, and hug, kiss, and pat each other's backs. They also feel grief and sadness. One adolescent chimp was so depressed after his mother's death that he wouldn't eat. He died just three weeks after she did.

- Chimps help other chimps and also humans. In one instance an adolescent chimp "adopted" a three-year-old chimp, taking good care of him after the baby's mother died. In another instance, an adult chimp came to the rescue of a human researcher who was being attacked by other chimps.

Jane experienced a turning point in her life and career in 1986 when she attended a conference of chimp researchers from around the world. She was shocked to learn that the chimp population in Africa had drastically declined for several reasons. Thousands of acres of rain forest had been cut down, which left chimps with no place to live and no food to eat. Chimps were also being hunted for food, called bushmeat. Orphaned babies were being sold as pets or for medical research. Jane was horrified by the terrible conditions chimps had to endure in research laboratories.

As a result, Jane's life mission changed. She became an activist rather than a researcher, and she committed herself to speaking out for chimps and their environment. While research at Gombe continues, Jane is only able to visit her beloved chimps a couple of times a year. As she said to this author in 2009, "Sometimes you have to leave the ones you love in order to save them." Her desire to help the chimps expanded to a worldwide mission that keeps her traveling over three hundred days a year.

The Jane Goodall Institute, which she founded in 1977, supports chimp research as well as habitat restoration and conservation programs that go hand-in-hand with chimp protection.

Jane's work also includes helping people. As she says, "How can we even try to save the chimpanzees and forests if the people are so obviously struggling to survive?" She started a successful program called TACARE to address poverty and support sustainable livelihoods in the villages around Lake Tanganyika. It's a model for community conservation that is being emulated in other places in the world.

"It is easy to be overwhelmed by feelings of hopelessness as we look around the world," she wrote in *Reason for Hope*. "We are losing species at a terrible rate, the balance of nature is disturbed, and we are destroying our beautiful planet... But in spite of all this I do have hope." Her hope is based on four factors.

Reason for hope #1: *The Human Brain*—Everywhere Jane goes she notices people making wiser choices and more responsible ones, such as recycling, electric cars, and solar energy.

Reason for hope #2: *The Resilience of Nature*—Resilience means the ability to recover. Jane has witnessed nature's ability to recover all over the world. An example is a tree in Nagasaki, Japan, that endured the atom bombing when it was a sapling. Although the tree is cracked on the outside and blackened inside, it still produces leaves.

Reason for hope #3: *The Determination of Young People*—Jane has a special interest in young people. She admires their tremendous energy, enthusiasm, and commitment. In 1991, a small group of high school students joined Jane at her home in Dar es Salaam, Tanzania. They told her that they wanted to do something to help animals, so Jane encouraged them to choose a project that helped their home villages. Jane then discovered that young people all over the world were like these Tanzanian students. They wanted to take positive action. In response, Jane created a youth program now called Jane Goodall's Roots & Shoots.

There are now groups of Roots & Shoots students from pre school through college in more than 120 countries. In Ohio, a group grows fresh vegetables for three gorillas kept at the zoo. In California, members study bees and learn how to help them survive. And in Australia, a group rescued 700 turtles from tubeworm infestation.

Reason for hope #4: *The Indomitable Human Spirit*—Jane is inspired by remarkable people she meets around the world. One example is Jon Stocking. He was a cook on a tuna fishing boat. One day Jon heard a baby dolphin crying. It was trapped in a net along with the tuna. When Jon made eye contact with the mother dolphin, she seemed to be pleading with him to save her baby. Despite the danger, Jon jumped into the water and lifted the baby dolphin out of the net to safety. Then he rescued the mother before cutting the net and freeing all of the captured tuna, sharks, and dolphins.

After that experience, Jon knew he wanted to make a difference to animals, so he started a chocolate company. For many years, ten percent

Jane observes rainforest wildlife in the Mamoni Valley Preserve in Panama in 2009.

of the profits from the chocolate sold went to support projects for species conservation, habitat, and humanity.

In 2009, Jane wrote *Hope for Animals and Their World*. The book is filled with stories of endangered species— condors, ferrets, wolves, frogs, and many more—being rescued from the brink of extinction by dedicated and caring people. Jane collected so many animal success stories they wouldn't all fit in the 400-page book, so she put these additional stories on a web site for all to read at www.janegoodallhopeforanimals.com.

Even in her mid-seventies, Jane spends most days speaking to government officials, environmentalists, or teachers and students about animal welfare, conservation, and world peace. A common question she hears is "What can I do to help?" Her answer: "There is a lot we can do, each and every one of us, just by trying to make the world around us a better place. It can be very simple: we can make a miserable dog wag his tail or a cat purr; we can give water to a little wilting plant. We cannot solve all the problems of the world, but we often do something about the problems under our noses." As it says on her web site:

> *Every individual matters.*
> *Every individual has a role to play.*
> *Every individual makes a difference.*

Jane never wanted to become a celebrity, yet she is famous throughout the world. Audiences greet her with the enthusiasm usually given to a pop star. She has received numerous awards and acknowledgments, including Disney's Animal Kingdom Eco Hero Award and The Kyoto Prize in Basic Science. She was made a Dame of the British Empire by His Royal Highness Prince Charles. Jane says,

> Perhaps one of the greatest honors I have ever received was being named a United Nations Messenger of Peace in 2002 . . . I carry the message that to achieve global peace, we must not only stop fighting each other but also stop destroying the natural world.

FAST FACTS

Born: April 3, 1934, in London, England

Married: Hugo van Lawick; Derek Bryceson

Son: Hugo, nicknamed Grub

ACCOMPLISHMENTS:
- Pioneered in the field of chimpanzee research
- Recognized as the world's leading authority on chimpanzee behavior
- Wrote twenty-four books for adults and children
- Discovered that chimpanzees use and make tools, disproving the theory that only humans make tools
- Championed the cause of animal rights and animal welfare
- Received worldwide honors, including UN Messenger of Peace

RIPPLES OF INFLUENCE:

Famous People Who Influenced Jane Goodall
Louis Leakey, Sir David Attenborough, Konrad Lorenz, Margaret Mead, Prof. Robert Hinde, her mother Vanne, her dog Rusty, and chimps David Greybeard and Flo

Famous People Influenced by Jane Goodall
Millions of people all over the world, including women scientists, environmentalists, animal researchers, educators, children, spiritual leaders, and indigenous people

TIMELINE

Jane Goodall's Life		Historical Context
	1929	E.O. Wilson born
	1933	Oria Douglas-Hamilton born
Born April 3	1934	
Receives Jubilee, chimpanzee toy	1935	
	1937	William Hornaday dies
Moves to The Birches	1939	World War II begins in Europe
Her parents divorce	1942	Iain Douglas-Hamilton born
	1945	World War II ends
	1949	First UN conference on environment
Moves to London for secretarial school	1952	
Takes first trip to Africa; meets Leakey	1957	USSR launches 1st satellite, Sputnik
Asked by Leakey to study chimpanzees	1958	
Begins Gombe chimp study; sees tool use	1960	
Receives first National Geographic grant	1961	
	1962	Carson writes *Silent Spring*; Darling dies
	1963	Kennedy assassinated
Marries Hugo van Lawick	1964	
Receives her Ph.D. from Cambridge	1965	First person walks in space
Son "Grub" born	1967	
Appointed to faculty at Stanford	1970	Saba Douglas-Hamilton born
	1972	U. S. government bans DDT
	1973	Endangered Species Act passed
Marries Derek Bryceson	1975	
Establishes Jane Goodall Institute (JGI)	1977	
	1979	Three Mile Island meltdown
Attends life-changing chimp conference	1986	
Creates Roots & Shoots	1991	
Establishes chimp sanctuary in Congo	1992	Earth Summit in Rio de Janeiro
Appointed U.N. Messenger of Peace	2002	
	2003	War in Iraq begins; R.D. Lawrence dies
	2006	*An Inconvenient Truth* released
Invested as Dame of the British Empire	2004	
Begins Earth Train partnership in Panama	2009	

The Douglas-Hamilton Family: Oria, Iain, and Saba

1933, 1942, 1970—present
A Family Saving Elephants

"Saving elephants is symbolic of something far greater—a future for the planet."

Saba grew up knowing that elephants were part of her family. She was only three months old when her mother, Oria, introduced her to her first elephant, Virgo, a one-tusked female.

Virgo was unique among wild elephants. She so trusted Saba's father, Iain, that she would actually touch him, nuzzling his hand with her trunk. Oria had earned Virgo's trust too, so she had no fear as the huge elephant approached her. But this meeting was different. How would Virgo react to Saba?

Oria stepped forward and stretched out her hand, offering Virgo a gardenia fruit in a gesture of greeting. Virgo grasped it with her trunk and put it into her mouth. Then she stretched out her trunk toward Saba, slowly moving it in a figure eight pattern over the baby's tiny body, smelling her. Virgo would remember Saba by her scent.

Then Virgo brought *her* baby forward, presenting her calf to Oria. With a shared understanding, the two mothers stood facing each other for a long while, their babies by their sides.

Being accepted by the world's largest land animal was an auspicious beginning for Saba, who grew up to become an elephant expert and a protector of wild animals. In many ways she has followed in her parents' footsteps. Her father, Iain Douglas-Hamilton, is one of the world's foremost authorities on elephants. Her mother promotes elephant awareness through writing and eco-safaris. Because of their research, the Douglas-Hamiltons relate to particular elephants as individuals, almost like extended family.

Saba's first job out of college was to work for Save the Rhino Trust in Namibia. Then in 1999 a BBC wildlife film producer "discovered" her. Saba quickly became a very public figure, hosting wildlife specials in the United Kingdom and producing films for *Animal Planet* in America. Millions of viewers have thrilled to her exciting adventures. She's faced charging rhinos, searched for tigers in India, tracked polar bears in the Arctic wilderness, and raced camels in the Sinai desert.

Not surprisingly, many of Saba's films feature elephants. In 2009, she teamed up with her father to make a remarkable documentary called *The Secret Life of Elephants*. This amazing film captures the hidden world of elephants by following the lives of several individual elephants. Saba describes some of the film's "main characters" this way:

> **Breeze**—a newborn calf whom we meet on her very first day of life, watch take her first shaky steps, and follow through the first challenging nine months of her life.
>
> **Buster**—Breeze's older brother. A bit of a "mummy's boy," he's initially jealous of Breeze. When he later develops an independent streak, he gets himself and his family into trouble.
>
> **Rommel**—a local legend! In the past he flattened one of our research vehicles, almost killing the two researchers who were inside. After a four-year absence he came back, bigger, badder and bolder than ever.

The film also highlights the dedicated work of Iain, Saba, and other researchers at Save the Elephants, a charity founded by Iain in 1993. Its goals are to protect elephants and preserve their habitat.

Iain's love for the wild animals of Africa began early in life. "If you had asked me at the age of ten what I wanted to do," Iain recalls, "I would have said . . . I want to fly around Africa and save animals." As a college student in 1965, he had his heart set on researching lions. But there weren't any open positions to study lions. Instead, Iain was offered the opportunity to research elephants, and he's been studying them ever since.

His research began at Lake Manyara National Park in Tanzania— a place that Ernest Hemingway called "the loveliest lake in Africa." The area around the lake was home to elephants, hippos, impalas, wildebeests, warthogs, giraffes, leopards, and lions.

At that time, the elephant population around Lake Manyara was increasing. Biologists wondered whether too many elephants would hurt the park's vegetation. Would the elephants wipe out the food supply for themselves and the other animals too? It was Iain's job to find out.

To find an answer, Iain had to determine how many elephants lived in the park, how many were born, and how many died over a period of time. But the elephants were constantly on the move throughout the reserve, and it seemed impossible to count them.

Other researchers had simply estimated the number of elephants in the park. That wasn't good enough for Iain. He wanted an exact count, so he devised an ingenious method to get it. Iain decided to photograph individual elephants and be able to recognize them by sight. No one had ever tried this before. He soon had photographs of hundreds of elephants and set to work identifying and memorizing their unique physical characteristics.

The first elephant Iain learned to recognize was a huge male elephant with a jagged tusk. Iain named him Cyclops. Because elephants use their tusks for digging, foraging, scraping or pushing trees, and sometimes for fighting, it wasn't unusual for Iain to see several animals with broken or even missing tusks.

Another distinguishing feature was an elephant's ears. An African elephant's ears are huge, much larger than those of an Asian elephant. Their overall shape, along with jagged edges, nicks, holes, and tears, provided many clues to an elephant's identity.

The most useful photos were those of elephants whose ears were spread out wide. But elephants typically displayed this posture when they were about to charge. Iain learned to quickly snap a photo and then run for his life with an angry four-ton elephant on his heels! He had many narrow escapes, especially from an excitable and combative group of elephants in the southern part of the park.

One day, while giving an American Peace Corps worker a close up view of elephants, an angry female attacked Iain's Land Rover. She plunged her long tusks into the vehicle, spinning it around. Then three more elephants joined in. Iain later wrote, "Tusks were thrust in and withdrawn with great vigour. Loud and continuous trumpeting rent the air, together with that fatal sound of tearing metal." A huge head caved in the roof. Another tusk punctured the radiator, and the "Land Rover was carried backwards at high speed for thirty-five yards until it squashed up against an ant heap surmounted by a small tree."

Nevertheless, Iain's method was successful. His photos revealed countless one-of-a-kind combinations of tusks and ears. Using photos and on-the-ground observations, he counted about four hundred elephants within the park. Iain named them all and began to understand how they interacted with one another as individuals.

However, it wasn't an elephant attack that put Iain into the hospital. It was a charging rhinoceros! It happened while Iain's mother was visiting. He had taken her on an excursion to see some interesting birds. As they followed a narrow path through dense undergrowth, Iain suddenly heard a loud snort. "Rhino! Run for it!" he shouted.

His mother escaped unharmed, but Iain was kicked and trampled. His back was severely injured. After being released from the hospital, Iain spent many weeks lying flat on the floor, completely immobilized. Not wanting to waste time, he made good use of his recovery by studying Kiswahili, the local language.

Once back on his feet and able to identify individual elephants, Iain made a discovery that surprised biologists. He determined that elephants form extended family units headed by a matriarch, an old and wise female. This female led her family of sisters, daughters, granddaughters, and young males to the best places to eat, drink, and rest. The average family consisted of ten elephants. Several family groups combined to form larger kinship groups of up to forty elephants.

Iain was also the first person to track elephants using radio collars. But putting a collar on an elephant is a tricky task. He went through a long process of trial and error before he perfected the technique. First he had to shoot an elephant with a tranquilizer dart and make sure it punctured the inch-thick skin. Then, working as fast as he could, Iain would wrap a large radio collar around the elephant's massive neck. Finally, he would give the elephant another injection to wake it up.

Iain, Saba, and the Save the Elephants team put a tracking collar on a tranquilized elephant.

It was a tense affair, with all kinds of unexpected difficulties. Many times other elephants protected the tranquilized one, keeping Iain from getting close enough to put the collar on. Iain worked as rapidly as he could so as to cause the elephants as little disturbance as possible. Now, with over forty years of experience, he and his team can collar an elephant in about four minutes from the moment it goes down to the moment the antidote is given.

At first Iain tracked the elephants' radio signals on a receiver in his Land Rover. But in 1969 he learned he could receive better signals from above. He acquired a small plane and flew exhilaratingly low over the park's diverse terrain, listening for elephants. He said he came to "know every square yard of the park from the air."

Iain loved flying. It was in his blood. His father had been a fighter pilot in WWII before he was tragically killed on a reconnaissance mission. Iain's three uncles were also fighter pilots, and one of them in 1930 gained the distinction of being the first person to fly over the top of Mt. Everest.

Iain's flying gave him the opportunity to win the heart of Oria Rocco, who became his wife. He first met Oria at a party in Nairobi, Kenya, in 1969. He couldn't wait to see her again, so he surprised her by flying out to her family farm in Kenya's Rift Valley. He caused quite a commotion on a quiet Sunday afternoon when he made a dramatic landing on their bumpy field.

The following day Iain flew Oria to Lake Manyara. She was fascinated by the work he did and his love for elephants. Most of the people Oria knew who lived in the bush were hunters. She had never met anyone who understood elephants so well and had so little fear of them. She also appreciated his adventurous spirit, maybe because she, too, was full of adventure. Oria soon moved to Lake Manyara, and together she and Iain studied and recorded elephant behavior.

Oria learned all she could about elephants. In the following passage she described an elephant's amazingly versatile trunk:

Partly lip and partly nose, with two fingers on the tip, it is used as a worker's arm and hand. It has double hoses for sucking in and spraying out water or dust, and can test the wind. It can push down trees or pick off the smallest leaf. It can be as gentle and as loving as the most tender arms . . . At the same time, it can change into an efficient weapon to kill, and when it detects the smell of man, rears back above the head like a serpent preparing to strike.

Based on their careful observations, Iain and Oria came to believe that elephants express a wide variety of emotions, including love, anger, jealousy, empathy, compassion and grief.

When Oria joined Iain at Lake Manyara, she learned all she could about elephants.

They react very strongly to dead or dying elephants, and will sometimes gather around a dead elephant's body, caressing it with their trunks and gently touching its tusks.

Oria and Iain wrote a book about their time at Lake Manyara called *Among the Elephants*. Oria concluded, "I was able to get a glimpse into the incredible complexity and sophistication that elephants show in their everyday activities. I not only learnt to understand and especially to respect them, I also longed to protect them." At that time she didn't know she and Iain would soon be mounting an all-out battle to save Africa's elephants from extinction.

Iain's five-year study ended in 1970, which was the same year Saba was born. Her name means "seven" in Kiswahili. She was born on June seventh, at seven o'clock, on the seventh day of the week, and is the seventh grandchild. Saba's sister, Mara, was born a year later. Oria describes both her daughters as "having sunshine in their hearts."

Saba and her sister had mongooses and genet cats as pets. Commenting on her early childhood in Kenya and Tanzania, Saba said, "Kiswahili was the first language we spoke, followed by English, and we hardly ever wore clothes. Mara and I ran wild in the African bush, climbing waterfalls and catching snakes."

One of the games Iain taught the girls was to quietly sneak up on an elephant and try to pull a hair out of its tail. "It was terrifying, insanely exciting, and something I would never do again!" stresses Saba.

When she was seven years old, Saba began school in the city of Nairobi. One of her favorite school memories is the day lions roamed onto the school's rugby field, canceling all sports for the rest of the afternoon.

It was during the girls' school years, the late-1970s and 1980s, that Iain and Oria realized that elephants were seriously under attack. They were being killed with automatic weapons, their tusks brutally hacked off to be sold, and the rest of the carcass left to rot. The human desire for ivory, Saba says, was causing an elephant "holocaust." Iain and Oria knew they had to do something to stop the ivory trade.

Iain began making aerial surveys of elephants in Kenya, Tanzania, and other African countries. Counting both living and dead elephants, his results were shocking. At the rate the elephants were being slaughtered, they would become extinct in Africa by 2015.

At first, he and Oria were alone in their fight against ivory poaching. Making great personal sacrifices, they risked their lives in skirmishes with poachers and spent long periods of time away from Saba and Dudu.

Flying over the Tsavo National Park in Kenya was a turning point for Saba as a young teenager. She saw whole families of elephants shot down by automatic weapons. She recalls, "We could smell them a thousand feet up . . . My parent's work influenced and inspired me enormously . . . They stood firm in the storm when everyone else was against them."

After a while, some other researchers and a few conservation groups joined the battle. The public eventually woke up to the problem when the media began showing photos of the rotting bodies of tuskless, dead elephants.

After years of contentious meetings, in 1989 the Convention on International Trade in Endangered Species (CITES) finally approved an international ban on the ivory trade. Mike Fay, a biologist and explorer, offered this praise for Iain in *National Geographic* magazine: "If there had been no Iain Douglas-Hamilton, there may never have been an ivory ban. Certainly the massacres would have continued for a longer time span."

Despite this victory, it was too late for hundreds of thousands of elephants. Between 1979 and 1989 over half of Africa's elephants had been killed. Iain and his family went back to Lake Manyara in 1990 to check on the elephants he had known so well. Of the four hundred elephants he had known in 1970, only three had survived the slaughter. Miraculously, Virgo was one of them, and Iain found her.

As Virgo stepped out of undergrowth, Iain spoke softly to her, hoping she would remember the sound of his voice. But Virgo was no longer the trusting elephant that had so tenderly greeted Saba as a baby. She and her family had endured years of hurt and suffering at the hands of humans. She looked at Iain for ten long minutes. Then she turned and disappeared into the bush. Although deeply disappointed, Iain knew her distrust of humans was for her own good.

A renewal of the ivory trade remains the greatest threat to elephants today. "Our battle with poachers is never-ending," Oria says. "Just when we think we are winning, we hear another elephant has been killed and his tusks removed." As recently as 2010, Tanzania and Zambia tried to remove the ivory trade ban and sell their stockpiled supplies. Fortunately, Iain and others successfully stopped their efforts.

Growing up among elephants, with parents so utterly dedicated to their preservation, Saba knew from an early age that she would live among animals and try to protect them. When Iain offered her a job at Save the Elephants (STE) in 1997, Saba eagerly joined him.

STE operates in the Samburu National Reserve in northern Kenya. About nine hundred elephants pass through the reserve; fifty or more family units make it their home, and about two hundred males roam more widely. Some STE staffers can identify five hundred elephants by name, including Breeze and her brother Buster.

The reserve is an essential safe-haven for elephants. As Africa's human population has expanded, elephant habitat has shrunk, causing clashes between people and elephants. STE has developed innovative solutions that ease some of the conflicts:

Saba grew up with elephants and has no fear of them. In addition to making wildlife films, she is also a Trustee for Save the Elephants.

- By outfitting elephants with special collars that use GPS and cell phone technology STE researchers receive location signals on their computers and cell phones. Reporter David Quammen joked that the elephants text, "Iain, yo, here I am." Seeing movement patterns helps STE develop safe wildlife corridors between protected areas.

- Elephants are really good at breaking down fences to get at farmers' crops. STE uses computer software to create "virtual fences." Whenever an elephant's collar signals that it is approaching a virtual fence line, rangers immediately drive out and chase it away. Elephants quickly learn not to return to that area.

- Elephants kill trees by stripping off bark and over-browsing. To save the trees, STE hangs hives in them. Angry bees drive away elephants that threaten their hives. Bee hive "fences" are now also used to stop elephants from raiding farmer's crops.

- STE believes "the best potential ambassadors for elephants are those who live amongst them, sharing their land and their future." Many of STE's researchers are Kenyans from Samburu, and STE works with local schools to give children a solid education and develop their elephant awareness.

The Douglas-Hamilton family has chosen a life of service to wildlife and people. They have each found their own special way to encourage others to serve.

Iain mentors the young researchers at STE. In turn, they teach and inspire others. One of his first research assistants at Lake Manyara, Cynthia Moss, now directs the Amboseli Trust for Elephants, a successful research and conservation organization. She, too, has produced television specials, including *Echo of the Elephants*.

Oria was inspired to create a safari camp, Elephant Watch Safari, for tourists near the STE research station. She used her artistic flair to establish a beautiful and exotic eco-lodge where people come from all over the world to watch elephants at close range. When the tourists return home they have a deeper understanding, appreciation, and respect for elephants. Many support the work of STE or sponsor a nomadic child's education.

Saba is a Trustee for STE and makes films about wildlife that both entertain and educate the public. Her engaging personality reaches out to audiences of all ages, teaching them about some of the world's remarkable animals. She believes strongly that if people love something they will do all they can to protect it. Like her parents, Saba lives in Africa with her husband and daughter.

Throughout their lives as conservationists, Iain, Oria, and Saba have faced daunting challenges—plane accidents, poaching, droughts, riots, and political unrest. A new challenge hit them in 2010—a flash flood. STE and Elephant Watch camps were completely destroyed. All of their equipment was washed away and some valuable research data lost.

Iain's passion for elephants comes from a deep respect, gained over forty years of observation and study.

"It's nothing short of a disaster," Iain said, "but we will take a deep breath and rebuild."

This kind of optimism and perseverance has led to many successful conservation efforts over the years. And it is reflected in Saba's words as she reminds people:

> Nature is what makes us whole; it is so valuable to our well-being that it is priceless. We still have time to save wildlife and wilderness, but we have to act fast . . . Each of us as individuals can make a difference.

[Editor's note: For a fascinating interview that the author had with Saba, go to www.dawnpub.com. The interview is posted on the web page for *Earth Heroes: Champions of Wild Animals*.]

FAST FACTS

Oria *Iain* *Saba*

Born
Oria: January 1, 1933
Iain: August 16, 1942
Saba: June 7, 1970

Married
Iain and Oria: 1971; daughters Saba and Mara; Saba to Frank Pope, 2006; daughter Selkie

ACCOMPLISHMENTS:
- Conducted a ground-breaking study on elephants that paved the way for future research and conservation (Iain)
- Pioneered innovative methods, such as photo identification and sophisticated tracking techniques (Iain and Oria)
- Alerted the world to elephant poaching crisis, resulting in an international ban on the ivory trade (Iain and Oria)
- Wrote *Among the Elephants* and *Battle for the Elephants* (Iain and Oria)
- Established a clinic that provides family planning and HIV/AIDS resources for 20,000 Kenyans (Oria)
- Produced and presented wildlife documentaries, including *Heart of a Lioness* and *Rhino Nights* (Saba)

RIPPLES OF INFLUENCE:

Famous People Who Influenced the Douglas-Hamiltons
Charles Darwin, Niko Tinbergen, Myles Turner, Bernard and Michael Grzimek, David Sheldrick, Jim Corbett, Jane Goodall, George Schaller, Winston Churchill, Blythe Loutit, and Dian Fossey, as well as their adventurous Scottish and Italian ancestors.

Famous People Influenced by the Douglas-Hamiltons
Cynthia Moss, Joyce Poole, Richard Leakey

TIMELINE

Douglas-Hamiltons' Lives		Historical Context
Oria born January 1	1933	
	1934	Jane Goodall born, Peterson's Guide
	1937	William Hornaday dies
Iain born August 16	1942	
	1945	World War II ends
	1949	First UN conference on environment
Iain's family moves to Africa	1952	
	1957	USSR launches 1st satellite, Sputnik
Iain begins Oxford University	1960	
	1962	Carson's *Silent Spring*; Darling dies
Iain goes to Serengeti Plains in Tanzania	1963	President Kennedy assassinated
Iain begins research at Lake Manyara	1966	
Iain and Oria meet	1969	
Saba born June 7	1970	EPA created
Iain and Oria marry; Mara born	1971	
	1972	U. S. government banned DDT
	1973	Endangered Species Act passed
Among the Elephants published	1975	
Saba begins school	1977	
Iain and Oria battle elephant poaching	1977-1989	
	1988	NASA warns of global warming
CITES bans ivory trade	1989	
Battle for the Elephants published	1992	Earth Summit held in Rio de Janeiro
Iain establishes *Save the Elephants*	1993	
The Elephant Family book published	1996	
Saba joins STE	1997	
Saba becomes a BBC wildlife presenter	1999	
Saba directs 1st film for *Animal Planet*	2003	War in Iraq begun; Lawrence dies
Saba marries Frank Pope	2006	*An Inconvenient Truth* released
The Secret Life of Elephants premieres	2009	
Selkie born		
Flood destroys STE and Elephant Watch	2010	

BECOME A HERO!

JUST DO IT!

Do what? Do what you love. Jane, Ding, and the other Earth Heroes didn't set out to change the world, they just pursued their interests.

Ed Wilson (*Champions of Wild Animals*) was hooked on ants. His curiosity about them eventually led to a scientific breakthrough about insect communication. Jacques Cousteau (*Champions of the Ocean*) fell in love with cameras and photography when he was a teenager. His interests eventually led him to make films about the ocean that introduced millions of people to undersea life.

Maybe frogs are your thing. Find the nearest pond or swamp, sit down and watch what happens. Henry David Thoreau (*Champions of the Wilderness*) spent an entire day at a little pond just watching the bullfrogs. Some people thought he was wasting his time, but his writings became the basis for the modern environmental movement.

What if you love dolphins, but don't live near the ocean? Not to worry. When Eugenie Clark (*Champions of the Ocean*) was nine, she couldn't go to the ocean either. So she became a regular visitor at her local aquarium. As an adult she swam with many of the fish she had observed in the aquarium's tanks. Jane Goodall (*Champions of Wild Animals*) loved chimps, but she lived in England, far away from them. But that didn't stop her. She learned all she could about African wildlife; and when the opportunity to go to Africa came along, she was ready to take advantage of it.

Follow your interests, whatever they may be. You may be surprised where they lead you—and the difference you're able to make.

BECOME A CITIZEN SCIENTIST

There is still so much to learn about wild animals. Scientists, especially those doing field studies, spend hours and hours observing and collecting data. Once the data is collected it has to be painstakingly analyzed. Oftentimes, there's just too much to do and not enough people to do it.

That's where you come in. Become a "citizen scientist." You can observe and collect information and send it to scientists. There are many different programs you can join. The information you collect might be about the birds in your area or the dates when trees flower. Here are just a few citizen science projects for you to check out:

- *Journey North* is an online global study of wildlife migration and seasonal change. Students K-12 report their own field observations. www.learner.org/jnorth
- *Project FeederWatch*, *Urban Birds Studies*, and *Great Backyard Bird Count* are just a few of citizen science projects sponsored by Cornell Lab of Ornithology. www.birds.cornell.edu
- *GLOBE* is a worldwide network of students, teachers, and scientists working together to study and understand the global environment. Schools can participate in GLOBE if at least one teacher gets trained in the GLOBE science measurement protocols. Training is free. www.globe.gov
- *Project BudBurst* invites members of the public to help scientists by collecting data about the timing of leafing and flowering in their areas. www.windows.ucar.edu/citizen_science/budburst
- *Monarch Watch* relies on volunteers across the United States and Canada. Individual butterflies are tagged and information is gathered to help scientists monitor monarch populations and the fall migration. www.monarchwatch.org
- *Firefly Watch* gives participants of all ages an opportunity to enjoy an annual summer evening ritual while helping scientists map the number and type of fireflies found in your area. www.mos.org/fireflywatch
- *Christmas Bird Count* is Audubon Society's early-winter bird census. Volunteers follow specified routes counting every bird they see or hear all day. www.audubon.org/bird/cbc
- *NatureWatch Canada* includes a suite of monitoring programs such as *FrogWatch*, *IceWatch*, *PlantWatch*, and *WormWatch*. These programs monitor soil, air, water, and other aspects of environmental quality. www.naturewatch.ca/english

JOIN JANE GOODALL'S ROOTS & SHOOTS

Jane Goodall designed the Roots & Shoots program especially for young people. If there's not a program near you already, you can start one. Through

Jane Goodall's Roots & Shoots you can design and implement three projects that you are specifically interested in, one for the local community, one for animals (including domestic animals) and one for the environment we all share. Whether you're passionate about polar bears, or serious about protecting bird habitat, Roots & Shoots gives you a way to get involved and make a difference.

The mission of Jane Goodall's Roots & Shoots is "to foster respect and compassion for all living things, to promote understanding of all cultures and beliefs and to inspire each individual to take action to make the world a better place for people, animals and the environment."

The power of youth is global: http://www.rootsandshoots.org

DISCOVER MORE HEROES

The three-book *Earth Heroes* series includes twenty-four biographies of men and women who have studied and protected the wilderness, ocean, and animals. We chose them for their diverse contributions, significant places in history, and inspiring personal stories. But there are hundreds more environmental heroes that aren't included in these books, and we encourage you to discover them. An Internet search will turn up more than a million Web sites related to environmental heroes. Your local library and book store are also great places to find fascinating biographies.

You may notice that men dominated the field of science until the mid-twentieth century. But the solid research of women such as Rachel Carson, Jane Goodall, and Eugenie Clark opened doors of opportunity for women scientists and environmentalists around the world.

Kids are environmental heroes too! Lynne Cherry, author of *The Great Kapok Tree* and *How We Know What We Know About Our Changing Climate: Scientists and Kids Explore Global Warming*, features some of them in her movie *Young Voices for Climate Change*. And according to Scholastic's Environmental Report Card poll, many kids believe that the real heroes include "Everyone who makes a difference in small ways." Find out who's making a difference in your world.

ABOUT THE AUTHORS AND ILLUSTRATOR

Bruce and Carol delight in animals of all shapes and sizes. Birds, deer, and raccoons are regular visitors to their home in the foothills of the Sierra Nevadas. On a recent trip to Panama they joined Jane Goodall in the rainforest where they were introduced to howler monkeys, toucans, and capybara. Bruce and Carol were educators for over 20 years, and they are honored that one of their former students, Anisa Hovemann, is the illustrator for this book.

Bruce and Carol have co-authored a series of teacher's guides for Dawn Publications. After several years of writing graduate courses for teachers, Carol now writes for a variety of audiences. In addition to the *Earth Heroes* series, she is the co-author for *The BLUES Go Birding* picture book series. Bruce continues to work with teachers as an educational consultant. Their current passions are birding, photography, and enjoying nature's beauty.

Anisa is a young artist with a fine sense of the human form. Her figures come alive with depth of character and expression. These black and white illustrations are based on careful research. She previously illustrated two full-color picture books, *If You Give a T-Rex a Bone* and *Eliza and the Dragonfly*. The latter was named Best Picture Book of the Year by the International Reading Association. Anisa is a graduate of the Maryland Institute College of Art. She lives near Seattle on the shores of Lake Washington where she paints and illustrates. Her art and illustrations can be seen at www.anisahovemann.com.

SOURCES AND CREDITS

WILLIAM HORNADAY

Andrei, Mary Anne. "The Accidental Conservationist: William T. Hornaday, the Smithsonian Bison Expeditions and the US National Zoo," *Endeavor* 29, no. 3 (September 2005) 109-113.

Dolph, James Andrew. "Bringing Wildlife to Millions: William Temple Hornaday the Early Years 1854-1896" (Ph.D. Dissertation, University of Massachusetts, 1975).

Robinson, Michael. "William Temple Hornaday: Visionary at the National Zoo." Smithsonian News Service (February 1989). http://nationalzoo.si.edu/AboutUs/History/hornaday.cfm

PHOTO CREDITS: p. 11, Rare Books and Special Collections, University of Rochester Library; p. 13, Smithsonian Institution Archives Record Unit 95, c 1880, Box 13, Folder 31-A; p. 15, Smithsonian Institution Archives Record Unit 95, c 1886, Box 13, Folder 39; p. 20, © Wildlife Conservation Society

JAY NORWOOD "DING" DARLING

Benjamin, Daniel K. "The Dust Bowl Reconsidered." *PERC Reports* 22, no. 4 (Winter 2004). http://www.perc.org/articles/article505.php

J. N. "Ding" Darling Foundation, http://www.dingdarling.org/

Lendt, David L. Ding: *The Life of Jay Norwood Darling*. 4th ed, Mt. Pleasant, SC: Maecenas Press, 2001.

The Papers of Jay Norwood "Ding" Darling. The University of Iowa Library, Iowa City, Iowa.

PHOTO CREDITS: all photos and cartoons from Special Collections, University of Iowa Libraries, courtesy of the "Ding" Darling Wildlife Society

RACHEL CARSON

Carson, Rachel. *Silent Spring*. New York: First Mariner Books, 2002.

Jezer, Marty. *Rachel Carson: Biologist and Author*. New York: Chelsea House, 1988.

Levine, Ellen. *Up Close: Rachel Carson*. New York: Viking, 2007.

The Life and Legacy of Rachel Carson, www.rachelcarson.org/

Wadsworth, Ginger. *Rachel Carson: Voice for the Earth*. Minneapolis: Lerner Publications, 1992.

PHOTO CREDITS: p. 41, 49, used by permission of the Rachel Carson Council; p. 51, Cover from *Silent Spring* by Rachel Carson (Boston: Houghton Mifflin Harcourt, 1962)

ROGER TORY PETERSON

Carlson, Douglas. *Roger Tory Peterson: A Biography*. Austin: University of Texas Press, 2007.

Devlin, John C. and Grace Naismith. *The World of Roger Tory Peterson*. New York: Times Books, 1977.

Roger Tory Peterson Institute of Natural History, http://www.rtpi.org/

Rosenthal, Elizabeth J. *Birdwatcher: The Life of Roger Tory Peterson*. Guilford, CT: The Lyons Press, 2008.

PHOTO CREDITS: p. 60, 66, and 68 Roger Tory Peterson Institute of Natural History; p. 63, Cover from *A Field Guide to the Birds* by

Roger Tory Peterson (Boston: Houghton Mufflin, 1939)

RONALD RD LAWRENCE

Cry Wild, http://crywild.com/

Lawrence, R.D. *The Green Trees Beyond: A Memoir*. New York: Henry Holt and Company, 1994.

Lawrence, R.D. *The North Runner*. New York: Ballantine Books, 1979.

Lawrence, R.D. *Secret Go the Wolves*. New York: Ballantine Books, 1980.

PHOTO CREDITS: All photos courtesy of Sharon Lawrence/The RD Lawrence Place

EDWARD O. WILSON

E.O. Wilson Biodiversity Foundation, http://www.eowilson.org/

Lord of the Ants. "NOVA." PBS. May 20, 2008. http://www.pbs.org/wgbh/nova/eowilson/

Moyers, Bill. "Bill Moyers Journal" PBS. July 6, 2007. http://www.pbs.org/moyers/journal/07062007/transcript1.html

Wilson, E.O. *Naturalist*. New York: Warner Books, 1995.

PHOTO CREDITS: p. 89 and 91, courtesy of Edward O. Wilson; p. 99, Mark Mahaney (courtesy of Edward O. Wilson), p. 100, Joe Pratt (courtesy of Edward O. Wilson)

JANE GOODALL

Goodall, Jane with Thane Maynard and Gail Hudson. *Hope for the Animals and Their World: How Endangered Animals are Being Rescued from the Brink*. New York: Grand Central Publishing, 2009.

Goodall, Jane. *My Life with the Chimpanzees*. New York: Aladdin Press, 1996.

Goodall, Jane. *Reason for Hope: A Spiritual Journey*. New York: Grand Central Press, 2000.

Greene, Meg. *Jane Goodall: A Biography*. Westport, CT: Greenwood Press, 2005.

The Jane Goodall Institute, http://www.janegoodall.org/

PHOTO CREDITS: p. 104, Jane Goodall Institute; p. 116, courtesy of Leah Jacobs, Buffalo, New York; p. 118, courtesy of Michael Neugebauer

DOUGLAS-HAMILTON FAMILY

Author Interview with Saba Douglas-Hamilton, 2010.

Douglas-Hamilton, Iain and Oria. *Among the Elephants*. New York: Viking Press, 1975.

Meredith, Martin. *Elephant Destiny: Biography of an Endangered Species in Africa*. New York: Public Affairs, 2001.

Quammen, David, "Family Ties: The Elephants of Samburu." *National Geographic Magazine* (September 2008). http://ngm.nationalgeographic.com/2008/09/samburu-elephants/quammen-text/1

Saba Douglas-Hamilton, http://www.douglas-hamilton.com/

Save the Elephants, http://www.savetheelephants.org/

PHOTO CREDITS: p. 125, Sam Gracey/©Save the Elephants; p. 127 and 134, Iain Douglas-Hamilton; p. 131, Simon Niblett/Saba Douglas-Hamilton; p. 133, Lisa Hoffner/©Save the Elephants; p. 134, Jake Drake-Brockman/©Save the Elephants, Lisa Hoffner/©Save the Elephants

INDEX

Africa 11, 65, 69, 103–106, 108, 110, 113, 119, 123, 128, 129, 130, 131, 132, 135, 136

Alabama 87, 89–91, 93–95, 100

Alaska 17, 19–20, 69

alligator 8

Amboseli Trust for Elephants 132

Audubon 56, 68

Audubon Club 55, 60

Audubon, John James 8, 10, 20, 36, 58, 68

Audubon magazine 58, 68 99

Audubon Society 14, 21, 37, 53, 56, 58, 65, 69, 137

bag limit 19, 21, 36

Beloit College 24

biodiversity 97, 98, 100, 141

bison 4, 13, 14, 15, 18, 19–20

Borneo 11–13

Boy Scouts 19, 20, 21, 56, 90–91

buffalo, see bison

Cambridge University 76, 119

Camp Chewonki 62, 63, 69

Canada 4, 18, 76, 78, 80–82, 84–85, 137

Carson, Rachel 4, 21, 38–53, 67, 68, 69, 84–85, 101, 119, 135, 138

Chatham College 43

citizen scientist 136–137

Clark, Eugenie 5, 136, 138

Convention on International Trade in Endangered Species (CITES) 129, 135

Cousteau, Jacques 84, 136

crocodiles 7, 8, 10, 12

Darling, Jay Norwood "Ding" 4, 21, 22–37, 53, 69, 85, 101, 119, 135–136

Darwin, Charles 8, 84, 100, 134

DDT 4, 39, 40, 50, 51–53, 66, 69, 85, 101, 119, 135

Douglas-Hamilton, Saba, Iain, Oria 4, 21, 37, 53, 69, 85, 101, 119, 121–135

Duck Stamp 33, 36–37, 69, 101

Earle, Silvia 5

ecology 5, 25, 48, 66, 75, 99–100

Encyclopedia of Life 98, 100–101

England 75, 77, 105, 118, 122, 136

entomologist 89, 90, 93, 94, 95

Clark, Eugenie 5, 136, 138

Florida 7, 12, 21, 35, 87, 92

Goodall, Jane 4–5, 21, 37, 53, 69, 84–85, 102–119, 134–139

Haliburton Forest and Wildlife Reserve 82, 84–85

Harvard University 90, 94–95, 101

Hornaday Medal 19

Hornaday, William 4, 6–21, 37, 53, 69, 85, 101, 119, 135

"hunt" birds with a camera 58

Iowa 8, 10, 23, 29, 30, 34, 36, 37

Iowa State University 10, 30

ivory trade 129, 130, 134, 135

Johns Hopkins 45

Kenya 5, 108, 126, 128, 129, 130

Lawrence, R.D. 4–5, 21, 37, 52–53, 69, 71–85, 119, 135

Leakey, Louis 109–111, 118–119

Leopold, Aldo 5, 14, 20–21, 30, 36–37, 84

Maathai, Wangari 5

Maine 49, 51, 62, 69

Maryland 45, 52

142   Earth Heroes: Champions of Wild Animals

Massachusetts 45, 63, 98

Mediterranean Sea 72, 74

Michigan 23, 36, 37, 82

Mississippi 87

Montana 13, 14, 15

Moss, Cynthia 132, 134

Muir, John 5, 14, 20, 21, 84

Murie, Margaret 5

National Wildlife Federation 19, 20, 34, 36, 47, 68, 101

New Caledonia 95

New Guinea 95

New York 10, 16, 17, 20, 29, 48, 59, 60, 61, 62, 67, 68, 69

Ontario 76, 79, 81, 82, 84, 85

orangutan 11, 12

ornithologist 57, 60-61, 63

Oskaloosa College 10

Pennsylvania 40, 43, 52

Peterson, Roger Tory 4, 21, 37, 52-53, 54-69

pheromone 96, 100

radio collar 125-126

Rivers School 63, 69

Roger Tory Peterson Institute 67

Roosevelt, Franklin 36

Roosevelt, Theodore 14, 20, 21, 26-27, 36, 52, 69

Roots & Shoots 115, 119, 137, 138

Save the Elephants 123, 125, 130-131, 135

Smithsonian Institution 8, 12, 15-16, 20

South Dakota 23-24

Spain 84

Suzuki, David 5, 52, 69

Tanzania 5, 110, 115, 123, 128-130, 135

taxidermy 9-13, 21

Thoreau, Henry David 21, 81-82, 84, 98, 136

Ward's Natural Science Establishment 10, 12, 21

Washington, D.C. 12, 16, 32, 88

wildlife refuge 5, 17, 30, 32, 33, 35-36, 37, 47, 51, 61

Wilson, Edward O. 4-5, 21, 37, 52-53, 64, 68, 69, 85, 86-101, 119, 136

Wisconsin 24

Wolf Centre 84

Woods Hole Marine Biological Laboratory 45-46, 53

Wyoming 32

zoos 17

Index   143

OTHER BOOKS FROM DAWN PUBLICATIONS

ALSO IN THE EARTH HEROES SERIES

Earth Heroes: Champions of the Wilderness features Henry David Thoreau, John Muir, Theodore Roosevelt, Aldo Leopold, Richard St. Barbe Baker, Margaret Murie, David Suzuki, and Wangari Maathai.

Earth Heroes: Champions of the Ocean features William Beebe, Archie Carr, Jacques-Yves Cousteau, Margaret Wentworth Owings, Eugenie Clark, Roger Payne, Sylvia Earle, and Tierney Thys.

FOR TEACHERS

Lesson plans for each book in the *Earth Heroes* series and suggestions for using them in your classroom are available at www.dawnpub.com under "Teaching Tools."

OTHER NOTABLE BOOKS

Girls Who Looked Under Rocks by Jeannine Atkins, illustrated by Paula Conner. The six women portrayed all grew up to become award-winning scientists, teachers, writers and artists.

John Muir: My Life with Nature by Joseph Cornell. This unique "autobiography" of John Muir is told in his own words, brimming with his spirit.

How We Know What We Know About Our Changing Climate: Scientists and Kids Explore Global Warming by Lynne Cherry and Gary Braasch. When the weather changes daily, how do we know that Earth's climate is changing? This book has won numerous awards. A separate Teacher's Guide by Carol L. Malnor offers lessons, resources, and guidelines for teachers.

Dawn Publications is dedicated to inspiring in children a deeper understanding and appreciation for all life on Earth. To review our titles or to order, please visit us at www.dawnpub.com or call 800-545-7475.